Reality Creation
101

ISBN: 1-4392-0004-1
ISBN-13: 9781439200049

Visit www.booksurge.com to order additional copies.

Reality Creation
101

Mastering Manifestation through Awareness

Christopher A. Pinckley

- Learn how to heal your unconscious
- Learn how to reprogram your neural net
- Understand the process of manifestation
- Learn how to release emotional wounds from the past
- Learn how to quit vicious cycles and self sabotage
- Become more powerful than you can possibly imagine
- Become self aware

≡ Contents ≡

Section Three: *Clearing and Healing*

Section Four: *The process of manifestation*

Contents

⇒ Foreword ⇐

I T IS MY great privilege to get to introduce you to "Reality Creation 101." It makes sense for me to do so, since bringing Christopher Pinckley into my experience was an act of manifestation.

After the success of the "Money Beyond Belief" program I did with Dr. Joe Vitale, I had requests for other programs, including one on creating the body of one's dreams. I was keen to do such a program, and I knew that the name would naturally be "Body Beyond Belief." But although I am in great health, I wanted to include the energy and presence of a collaborator with a better knowledge of physical fitness to help me create this program.

Enter Christopher Pinckley... "as if by magic."

It was icing on the cake that, not only is Chris an expert fitness trainer, he is also no stranger to the Law of Attraction. That is evidenced in this book you are now reading.

I have to admit that there was some expanse of time between Chris' request that I write this foreword and when I actually found the time to read this book. When I finally got around to it, I had to apologize for the delay. Not just to Chris — but also to myself, for having waited so long to allow myself the pleasure I got from reading this manual.

As a global society, we have certainly manifested a few books on the subject of... well, manifesting. What I enjoyed about this one is how personal it is. It doesn't read like a book that's full of just nice theories — Chris teaches from his experience. This isn't information just handed down from on high — it was discovered in the trenches of real life. I appreciate that opportunity to relate — even though the details of each of our experiences may differ. And rather than just telling stories, he then provides practical steps to help you make the same advancements he achieved.

It would be easy to say I loved this book because Chris just wrote a bunch of things with which I agree — that this is a book of my own already-established beliefs — but that wasn't the case. Chris' thoughts and ideas often challenged me. Sometimes the differences were a matter of semantics — sometimes there were ideas that I hadn't considered, or even conflicted with some ideas I had. That challenge promoted expansive thinking, for which I am grateful. I kept a pad of paper beside me, and wrote pages of notes as thoughts went flying. At times it was almost a struggle to keep reading because I felt so inspired to run out and take action!

I could try to list the parts of the book that I really enjoyed, but it would just end up looking like the table of contents, so I'll leave it to you to discover what will most speak to you. The Law of Attraction is at work in our lives. The potential for the life you desire exists all around you. I am confident that this book will help you in your journey to harness your inner strength and wisdom to create the life of your dreams. After all, isn't that why you manifested it into your experience in the first place…?

Be Magnificent!

Brad Yates
Author of "The Key to Success" and co-author of "Freedom at
    Your Fingertips"
Antelope, CA
April 2008

≋ Acknowledgments ≋

THERE ARE SO many wonderful people that I would love to thank for helping me both with the book and on my own path of evolution in consciousness.

Thanks to my three test readers, James, Rod, and Brenda for taking the time out of their busy schedules to read my book. Their contributions were invaluable in making my book accessible to the reader.

I would like to thank Brad for being a friend and a mentor. His gentle tutelage and wise words have continued to give me the validation and support necessary to become more than I was the day before, and to have the courage to finish writing this book.

A special thanks to my friends Mark and Irene for giving me the tough love that I needed to keep on writing!

Thank you to all of the wonderful self-help writers out there who I drew knowledge, technique, and inspiration from.

Finally, I would like to thank my editor Lisa Zure. Without her, this would never have become an actual book. She was there, not only to coach me, but also to help establish the message that I wanted to relay to the reader. There is no way that I could have done this without her.

➥ Introduction ☙

A T THE BEGINNING of his great work, *The Road Less Traveled*, M. Scott Peck shares a simple yet profound truth: "Life is Difficult." My life was extremely difficult. The harder I tried, the harder it got. The more I struggled, the more I strained. I pushed with everything I had to get things done, to achieve the goals I'd set for myself. Life pushed right back. In the midst of my misery, I often wondered if there might be a better way. It was obvious that I was going nowhere fast; working for sub-minimal pay, doing jobs I couldn't stand, getting into no-win relationships, and drawing confrontational people to myself on a regular basis.

Because of my unhappiness with my work situation, I was constantly sabotaging myself and getting fired. Eventually, I reached the point of total exhaustion. I could barely pick myself up out of bed in the morning. Every day it was always the same thing, just trying to get ahead. Just like my dad, just like my mom. I loved them both very much, but Good Lord! I didn't necessarily want to follow in their footsteps! I considered my parents to be a couple of hard-working folks—the only problem was, they weren't hardworking by choice.

My intimate relationships fared no better. I ended and began new relationships as often as I got fired and hired at various jobs. Some of my friends had wonderful relationships and seemed so happy. *Why couldn't I achieve that?* My relationships had a tendency to end in yelling matches or some other sort of dysfunctional behavior. I'd get into relationships, only to find myself ultimately feeling very powerless, or jealous, insecure, or bored. It was easy to blame the various women I dated for my relationship problems, and I felt totally justified in doing so. But I found out that blaming other people for your own problems doesn't help you transcend them.

Time passed, and I continued to bounce around between different jobs. I worked at a telemarketing firm for many years and even got promoted to management there. It was fun, but paid very little. I worked all kinds of odd jobs, including mailroom attendant, customer service rep, bartender (my personal favorite), waiter, bouncer, dancer, and a variety of others. I remember my very first job in my hometown of Fayetteville, Arkansas, at Mr. Burger. I started at $3.35/hr and earned two nickel raises during the first year, ending at $3.45/hr. I was damn proud of my raises, even though it was disgusting work that involved draining the grease from the fryers every night. I would come home smelling like grease, fries, and grilled meat.

As I got older, I began to understand that whatever I was doing, wasn't working. I'd gained enough wisdom to realize, *I know that I don't know.* I didn't know why things were the way they were. I didn't know why I couldn't get it together. I didn't know how to get where I wanted to be, which happened to be the exact opposite of where I was.

In addition to the conundrum of moneymaking, there was the ongoing issue of my emotional instability and personal relationships. Why did I always give my power away in relationships and why did I seem to draw confrontation to myself wherever I went? I struggled to maintain any sort of healthy intimate relationship as I vainly tried to figure out why people reacted to me the way they did. I think it may have had something to do with the fact that I had a tendency to handle life situations the same way I'd handled them when I was thirteen years old. But, why did I do *that*?

Then one day it happened. Driven to desperation, I hit the bookstore. I can't even tell you how I wound up in the self-help section, except perhaps that I knew I needed help. I picked up one of the first best books I have ever read to this day. It was *The Power of Your Subconscious Mind* by Dr. Joseph Murphy. After I read that book, I literally transformed. This was the first book that actually put the power back into my hands—into my mind. I began to understand how people can purposefully, *using their minds and their thoughts*, create their lives. It was here, for the first time, that I began to realize I could really do whatever I wanted to do. I became hungry for more knowledge, more empowerment. I read an entire barrage of books including The Road Less Traveled, The Nature of Personal Reality, and Many Lives, Many Masters. From that point on, my life transformed and I enjoyed the beginnings of purposefully creating my life to be the way *I wanted it to be.*

You, too, can do this. If your life has been hard, or even extremely difficult, you can still create your dreams. There are no quick fixes, but there is a radical change in perspective that can literally alter your life in a matter of days. When I see people struggling and toiling, my heart aches; I know what that's like, I've been there. When it seems like you're up against the wall with nowhere to turn and your time is up—yeah, I've been there.

But I'm not there anymore. What I've discovered is this: *You can create your life exactly the way you want it to be, no questions asked and no forms to fill out. There are no prerequisites to this. You do not have to earn it, you do not have to deserve it, and you do not have to prove yourself to anyone ever again. You just have to want it, that's all.*

This book was written to give you the tools you'll need to transform your life into a joyful experience that continually fulfills your brightest dreams. The process of creating your dream life only requires that you be honest with yourself, that you apply yourself with dedication and consistency, and that you be willing to cultivate self-awareness. The more self-awareness you have, the easier it will be to master your Reality Creation. Yes, it will take some work and an open mind, but I promise you, the results will be well worth effort.

Some may find that this book offers minor course corrections as they continue on their journey to manifesting their heart's desire. Others will find that it helps to lift them out of the dark places that unnecessarily held them back; elevating them to a road of light-hearted joy and fulfillment. Many will find that it completely alters their lives, offering them the total creative freedom and self-empowerment to truly live the life they've always wanted. This is just an opening, one of many along the road. I provided this opening to appeal to those people that are tired of feeling powerless to create what they want in life. This opportunity is for you.

May you create the life of your dreams!

Christopher A. Pinckley
Oakland, California
May, 2008

Section One: An Overview

"The state of grace is a condition in which all growth is effortless, a transparent, joyful acquiescence that is a ground requirement of all existence." —Seth

The Nature of Personal Reality, by Jane Roberts

≋ 1 ≋

What is Reality Creation?

EVERYONE HAS THEIR PROBLEMS, but some people seem to struggle with their problems a lot less than others. Why is this? If you have ever met anyone who enjoys living life on their own terms, as opposed to struggling with the "inevitable" challenges so many of us take for granted, that person has most likely discovered the key to mastering their *Reality Creation*. This key is *self-awareness*. As you become self-aware, you will no longer make the same choices over and over that continually recreate the same unwanted results in your life. The more self-aware you become, the more you are able to master your Reality Creation. The more you master your Reality Creation, the more you can begin to chart a course for your life that truly reflects the peace and fulfillment you desire.

We create our own reality—that is just a fact. Your Reality Creation is the sum total of every aspect of your life at any given moment. It includes everything in your life you *do want*, as well as those things in your life you *don't want*. Every material thing, situation, person, and experience could be considered part of your Reality Creation. Your Reality Creation also encompasses every facet of your beingness; this includes all of the various energies you are constantly emitting. You see, you are always sending out a great barrage of signals into the environment. Some of these signals you may be aware of, such as your conscious thoughts, words, emotions, and many of the actions you take. However, you may have no awareness whatsoever of the unconscious signals you are sending into your life or the associated actions you take. Simply stated, your Reality Creation is the culmination of **all** the energy you are putting out into the Universe; conscious *and* unconscious, positive *and* negative. This functions as a set-point that governs what you are continually magnetizing to yourself, regardless of whether or not you are trying to create a specific result in your life. *By mastering your Reality Creation, you will be mastering the set-point for the overall and ongoing quality of your life.*

Here's how it works: Everything that happens in your life, everything you draw to yourself and everything you do, is a manifestation of your thoughts. Whether you are aware of it or not, you thought it before it happened. Your thoughts are fueled by the emotional patterns and belief systems in your vibrational field. Also known as your bio-energetic field, or the energy in and around your body, your vibrational field is comprised of your conscious and unconscious emotions, thoughts and belief systems, as well as the signals that emanate from them. Taken a step further, your vibrational field determines your vibrational rate of attraction, which, in turn, determines the types of experiences and situations you magnetize into your life. If you are unsure about your vibrational rate of attraction, you can always look at what you are physically drawing to yourself. If you are drawing to yourself people, places, and circumstances that feel good, you are probably on track. Otherwise, you may need to do some work to enhance your Reality Creation and elevate your vibrational rate of attraction.

Obviously, one of the most important aspects of Reality Creation is your ability to purposefully manifest specific desired outcomes. To manifest something means to bring it from the nonphysical into the physical, utilizing spiritual energy. This can be something as seemingly ordinary as manifesting a parking place, to manifesting something more miraculous, like your soulmate or your dream job. The Art of Manifestation, then, is the ability to harness spiritual energy to create specific things in your life on command. The more self-aware you become—the more aware you are of your emotional states and beliefs—the more you will be able to utilize this Art. Truthfully, you are utilizing this amazing ability every second of every day of your life; it's a matter of becoming aware that you are doing so in order to consciously command it. This ability has always been with you, just waiting for you to claim it through your conscious awareness of its existence. In other words, you are already a Master of Manifestation, now all you have to do is to *consciously* use the power within you to create the results you desire.

What is power? Power is merely the ability to give yourself choices or options in life. You may have noticed that the fewer options you have, the more powerless you feel. Conversely, the more options you are able to create for yourself—the more choices you are able to make—the more powerful you feel. It feels good to have choices and options, and that good feeling comes from true power. How do you achieve this power? The road to ultimate power, or *empowerment*, comes from obtaining self-awareness and developing a true understanding of how you have been creating your life.

Many people make the mistake of associating power only with large sums of money. In truth, if you had not first cultivated some inner sense of empowerment, you would never have any money, whatsoever. Taken a step further, you could say that money is only one facet of the total reflection of how powerful you feel. Other facets could be your relationship, your physical body, your intellect, your career, and your spirituality or connectedness. How much power do you allow yourself to have? In fact, all these aspects of your life are only outer reflections of your inner sense of power. They will manifest physically in your life according to the feelings and beliefs you hold about yourself. In this way, you are constantly manifesting your reality based upon your own inner blueprint of conscious and unconscious emotions and beliefs. Generally speaking, most people are not purposefully manifesting things in their lives, but rather manifesting by default based upon the unknown wilderness that lies within them.

Wouldn't you like to have total control over your life? I personally struggled with understanding how to utilize the Art of Manifestation for years. I tried many different approaches, most of which brought some tangible results, but nothing lasting or fulfilling. I suffered many agonizing defeats, as well as near homelessness, while trying to manifest my dream life. Only after many years of struggle and strife, years of application and research, was I finally able to understand and successfully utilize what I had learned.

The first thing I did was to apply my new understanding of manifestation to my personal training and rehabilitation business, which was floundering at the time. The results were profound. Very quickly, I was booked solid with clients, and have remained so ever since. From the moment I gleaned a true understanding of how to manifest, I have never needed to do any additional advertising or marketing for my business. On top of that, I was able to create more fulfilling business and personal relationships than I'd ever had, and finally begin the healing process of my overworked, broken body.

Because of my studies, research, and applications, I was able to help effect rewarding, fulfilling, and lasting changes in my own life, as well as in the lives of my clients. *I discovered that when you really understand the principles involved in manifestation, you can literally create whatever you want.* However, most people face a multitude of stumbling blocks on the road to unlocking their creative freedom. Because I have worked through many of these blocks in my own life, I understand that there are elements missing from the traditional approach to manifestation and that most people are unaware of what these missing elements are. This is critical, because the missing elements are the keys to help you understand why you create what you do *not* want. *Understanding how you create what you do not want is a major step to clearing the way so that you can create what you do want.*

As I successfully mastered the Art of Manifestation, I began to realize that there was still something missing from my life. Even though I had now manifested a better job, a more fulfilling relationship, a nicer home and more income, I still had a deep inner sense of discontentment. And I still felt that I was struggling to overcome some unperceived obstacles that appeared to be surfacing from some mysterious place inside of me, interrupting the overall quality of my life. It was this feeling of unrest that led me to investigate the true nature of Reality Creation. When I began to look at the larger picture of my Reality Creation, instead of only just at the specific outcomes that I was attempting to manifest, I became even more powerful, and the overall quality of my life vastly improved. In this book, I will share with you my personal life lessons, along with the teachings that have been passed on to me, so that you, too, will be able to manifest whatever it is your heart desires and master your Reality Creation.

≡ 2 ≡

A New Approach
to the Art of Manifestation

THE BIG QUESTION is this: *If anyone at any moment can use the Art of Manifestation to create their reality, why isn't everyone doing it?* The answer is that everyone *is doing it*; they are just unaware of this fact. What makes this truth difficult to grasp is the time delay between your habitual thoughts, words, deeds and the actual physical manifestation of their effect on your life. Until you realize that you are *literally standing in the midst of yesterday's thoughts about your reality today, you will not understand that it was you who created it.*

We are constantly projecting our reality outwards, from this moment, into the future, and constructing it anew. This truth becomes a prison when you have trouble redirecting your habitual negative thought patterns and/or discarding your unwanted emotional baggage; you will continue to create the same distressing reality over and over. However, this truth can be Heaven on Earth when you learn how to take charge of your thoughts, emotions and words — when you embrace the ability to create your dream life.

Everyone has within them an Inner Master who can manifest whatever they want at any time. *The path to Mastery is merely the work of revealing that you have always been a Master.* The moment you become consciously aware of the fact that you are already manifesting your reality, you can begin to change it. Learning to manifest whatever you want in your life will motivate you to take full responsibility for your thoughts, words, and deeds. Many people around the world have already learned how to unlock their inner power and create amazing things that bring positive changes into their lives. However, there are still people who, although they have heard about or tried to utilize the Art of Manifestation, have not been able to effect the changes they desire. These are people who:

- ❧ Don't believe
- ❧ Are skeptical
- ❧ Are spiritual burnouts (tried it all, been there done that)
- ❧ Want to believe but can't
- ❧ Have tried it and failed
- ❧ Feel trapped in a vicious circle
- ❧ Are depressed and lonely and don't have the foggiest idea of where to begin

- Are living in such poverty consciousness that manifesting what they want seems like winning the lottery
- Don't dare to dream because it hurts to think about what you believe you can't have
- Are just trying to make a living
- Live in war-torn countries
- Are just unhappy and don't know why
- Feel like they have it all but are still missing something
- Feel unworthy and undeserving
- Are trapped in co-dependent situations
- Just can't decide what they want to do with their lives
- Are physically depleted and don't have any energy left to do anything about it

Obviously, the idea of manifestation is not new. What makes this book different is that I will give you *all* the steps required to master your Reality Creation. Regardless of whether you are familiar with the concept of manifestation or are just hearing about it for the first time, this book will empower you to *successfully create* the reality you desire. *I am offering you the option to do, be and experience something beyond what you have thus far experienced in your life.* You will be provided with the missing links for understanding how to manifest your life exactly the way you want it. You will understand how you have created your life the way you have thus far—how you have created your joys, as well as how you have created your sorrows. You will gain clear insight into how you've created the circumstances in your life; even how you have drawn the people into your life with whom you interact. You will ultimately come to understand what a powerful creator you are and how to wield this power to create only that which your heart desires.

≋ 3 ≋

Infinite Power
Equals Infinite Manifestation

T HERE IS AN inherent power in every living thing and in every single thing in the entire Universe. The Vedic Seers call it "Chita," or subtle matter energy. The Taoists call it "Chi," or life force energy. The ancient Mayans call it "Manna," or magical energy. Many independent spiritualists refer to it as "Source Energy." Quantum physicists call it "potential" or "latent energy." Whatever the case, there is a common consensus amongst many spiritual practitioners and scientists that there exists an inexhaustible supply of energy that we can somehow tap into. Further, they acknowledge that there is a unified force behind the creation of all things in physical existence. "Manifestation" is the act of bringing non-physical energy into the physical. The "Art of Manifestation" is the ability to utilize this energy to create whatever you want in your life whenever you want to. You were born with this ability and you can use it to consciously rearrange, transform, or completely change yourself and your life in any way you can conceive of. *The Art of Manifestation is utilizing the very Power that created the Universe itself.* When you tap into this Power, you can harness the energy of a tidal wave to create your dreams. This means that you are utilizing non-physical energy to do the greater part of the work for you in manifesting your pursuits. You, yourself, will always need to take some sort of physical action. However, the more adept you become at utilizing the Art of Manifestation, the less physical action you will be required to take.

The great illusion is that there is eventually an end to the amount of things we can create. The reality is that there is no end to the amount of potential energy existent within the Universe. One thousand Earths with over six billion people on each one couldn't put a fractal dent in the amount of energy available for manifestation. The competition for resources perpetuates this great illusion, driving the masses onwards to out-strive one another in order to have enough to survive. When you begin to really and truly grasp the concept of manifestation, all fear of lack, competition, survival, and limited resources will fall away. Once you have begun utilizing your power, you will always have everything that you need. The road to Mastery is complex, interwoven with limiting beliefs, emotional trauma, conditioned behavioral patterns, the Mass Mind beliefs or belief systems of all the people around you, and your own personal set of goals, dreams, and desires. But Mastery is attainable. As I have said, it is only a matter of revealing the Master that is already within you.

A great way to gauge your progress in life is to simply ask yourself, "Have I done everything I want to do? Do I have everything I want to have? Am I truly happy?" A Master of Manifestation, or you might say the *Master Creator,* has manifested everything in their life they want, with no repressed desires, hidden ambitions, or unmet needs. Most people who read this book are doing so because they are already well aware that there are many things they wish to accomplish or experience. Even if you still have things you want to do— indeed, even if you have not experienced *any* of the things you want to experience— you are still on your journey to Mastery. All the possibilities lay ahead.

Even when you have become a Master Creator, you will not be done creating; it's simply that you won't have any hidden desires or unmet needs. This means that when a desire arises spontaneously, you immediately set about the process of manifesting it. At this level of awareness, after having worked through the unhealed emotional wounds and issues within yourself, your desired manifestation will manifest simultaneously with the desire.

I have personally seen people who live their lives this way. They have done the necessary emotional clearing work on themselves to the point that, as soon as they conceive of a desire, it has already manifested in the physical. For these people, life is a continuous magical fluid moment of *nowness*. Can you imagine not having a single worry in your life ever again?

Before I actually met anyone who could do this or, even better, *lived it*, I conceptually understood the idea that one could spontaneously manifest their heart's desire. However, it would be many years before I could bridge the gap between my ability to intellectualize this concept versus actually being able to apply it in my life.

On my journey of self-discovery, I have met many people who paid great lip service to the intellectualization of spiritual power. However, few of these people were actually living the concepts they were preaching— myself included. On the other hand, I have also met many great teachers along the way who would admit that they were very much still human and working on themselves just as much as the next person. These are the teachers who I came to respect and understand the best. They did not put themselves on a pedestal or hide behind a façade of inhuman perfection. They would readily and openly acknowledge their weaknesses, as well as their strengths. Their message to me was that every single person you meet is still working on *something*. What this meant to me is that the only true Guru is the Guru within yourself.

≡ 4 ≡

Your Vibrational Energetic Field

A S WE'VE DISCUSSED, every human being has an energetic field surrounding them. This field is composed of the various energies in their mental, emotional, physical, and spiritual bodies. The biggest contributing factor to your energetic field, or rather the most controllable factor, is your emotional energy body. Your emotional energy body, to a large degree, can determine the overall rate of your vibrational field. This is important because your vibrational field determines your vibrational rate of attraction or what you are *magnetic to*. Lower emotions, such as anger, fear, depression, jealousy, and so on, are also vibrationally lower in nature. Higher emotions, such as joy, happiness, love, enthusiasm, and inspiration, are vibrationally higher in nature. The more control you have over your emotional state of being, the more control you have over your vibrational magnetism.

Your vibrational energetic field extends outwards around and away from you, affecting everything in your environment. This energetic field is most powerful in your immediate environment and diminishes the farther out it gets from *you*: its source. You are constantly radiating this energy wherever you go, whether you are aware or unaware of it. *In other words, you are constantly emitting a signal and either positively affecting or negatively infecting the environment and people around you.* When two people are in a room together and one is emitting a lower vibrational energetic field, while the other is emitting a higher vibrational energetic field, the two energies will conflict. Whoever has the stronger energetic field will win out. One of these two people will begin to feel very uncomfortable and leave the room. The other option is that the person emitting the weaker energetic field will assume the same vibration of the person emitting the stronger energetic field. A great fallacy is that positive energy, just because of the fact that it is positive, is stronger than negative energy. The fact of the matter is that someone can emit negative, lower vibrational energy that is just as powerful as positive energy.

If you are feeling happy and upbeat and walk into a room with someone who is in a bad mood, you may notice several things. First, you are keenly aware of their bad mood because it is in direct opposition to your own vibrational field. Second, the more time you spend next to them, the more you notice that you may become infected with their lower vibrational energetic field. In fact, it may take considerable effort for you to remain unaffected by their lower vibrational field of influence and you may start feeling yourself getting into a bad mood. If you become infected with their lower vibrational energetic field, you may then leave the room in a bad mood. In this vibrationally altered state, you are now magnetic to other people with lower vibrational fields, as well.

Conversely, if you were in a great mood and feeling powerful in your energetic field, you can positively affect all of the people around you. You can elevate all of the other people's energetic fields around you with your powerful energy. If you can do this purposefully, then you will become magnetic to higher vibrational people, places, and circumstances. Generally speaking, people that are good at this have healthy bodies, full bank accounts, and great relationships with their mates.

It is important to understand that there is a strong difference between *acting* positive and upbeat versus really *feeling* positive and upbeat. In other words, I have met many people who outwardly appear cheery and happy, but are inwardly angry, sad, or depressed. This is also reflected in their outer experience. You may be able to hide your emotional state physically, but you cannot hide the energy that you are putting out. So, if you are feeling negative inside, but acting outwardly positive, you will still draw to yourself negative circumstances. You may even trick yourself into thinking that you are really happy, even though you are not, and then wonder why your life is so crappy.

This is completely different from someone who is actually feeling negative and decides to "fake it until they make it." *Choosing to focus on something positive is a great way to effect change in your life, as long as you are not repressing your unhealed emotional energy.* For example, when my shoulder injury was out of control I used to get into a bad mood even before I got into the gym. I absolutely loved working out, but absolutely hated the fact that I couldn't work out very efficiently with a massive shoulder injury. While working out, I was constantly faced with the embarrassment of working out next to other guys who were in better shape than I was physically. My bad mood didn't stem from the fact that they were in better shape than me, but rather from the fact that I used to be in great shape myself. Outwardly I appeared very cheery and happy, but inwardly I was angry and frustrated that life was so easy for these guys. They could just come into the gym, play around with a few weights, and look great. I, however, had to struggle and strain to get any kind of gains on account of my wicked injury. As a result of this, I would get nasty looks from other guys in the gym all the time. I was so negative about my situation that I was sending out my angry vibes to everyone around me in the gym. Putting on the happy face didn't work.

What I decided to do instead was actually visualize myself being very physically fit, as well as to send out silent blessings to all of the guys in the gym who looked like I wanted to look again. It wasn't easy, but at least I wasn't angry in the gym anymore. And, of course, magically, people in the gym began behaving a lot nicer to me. Coincidentally, my workouts got better and better over time. It wasn't the end answer to my shoulder injury, but it made my workouts in the gym more enjoyable, while at the same time creating a more positive environment around me.

If you feel like it's going to be a terrible day, but instead find something to focus on that makes you happy, you may actually be able to turn your day around. Better than that, you will also elevate your vibrational field and your vibrational rate of attraction, becoming magnetic to other higher vibrational people, places, and circumstances. Anyone can do this; it is just a matter of making the choice to get started and then being consistent to effect change.

⪰ 5 ⪯

The Process Broken Down

Broken down to its basic elements, the Art of Manifestation is incredibly simple. You simply use the following model:

1) Decide what you want and state it out loud as an intention to manifest it.
2) Let it go, giving allowance for it to come to you in its own time and its own way.
3) Act on the lead that the Universe brings to you.

This seems really straightforward and easy to understand, doesn't it? You might even think it seems too good to be true. The fact is, when this process is utilized concisely, with no mental or emotional resistance, manifestation will take place just that easily. I have utilized it for myself and seen miracles happen in my life. I have also helped others to utilize their own latent power and create miracles for themselves, as well. It's exciting to watch people make huge changes in their lives in a matter of days. Sometimes these changes are so big that nobody would have ever believed it was possible.

However, many people have tremendous mental and emotional resistance to this process. *Your resistance will generally come in one of two forms. No matter what else it seems to be, your resistance will either be in the form of **beliefs** or **emotional trauma**. Every other form of resistance you could think of probably stems from one of these two areas.* They are both complex areas and make up the majority of how you create your reality and why you create it. Some people can create what they want despite their mental and emotional blocks. Unfortunately, many people have a tough time hurdling these inner blockages and never get to create what they really want. Trapped in a vicious cycle, life becomes a boring, or worse, depressing routine. Life is never fun when you are *living to survive*. We should all have the opportunity to *live life to enjoy ourselves and have fun*!

Thus, I have created a new process for mastering, not only manifestation, but, more importantly, your Reality Creation. This process entails all of the additional steps needed to make sure you are able to create what you want. The new model addresses the difficulties and challenges people face, and teaches them how to hurdle these perceived obstacles. The steps to mastering your Reality Creation are:

1) Understand how you created your life.
2) Clear yourself of inner blockages.
3) Get clear about what you want.
4) Manifest your dream life.

I have broken this book down into four basic sections to facilitate the process of mastering your Reality Creation. These are:

Section One: *An Overview*
Section Two: *Why People Have Trouble Manifesting*
Section Three: *Clearing and Healing*
Section Four: *The Art of Manifestation*

It may be helpful to reread certain sections to reinforce some of the concepts and principles presented in this book. If you begin to apply even one of the principles in this book, you will experience a dramatic shift in the way in you create your reality. You may even begin to take control of your Reality Creation and learn how to master the Art of Manifestation.

Section Two: Why People Have Trouble Manifesting

"There would be no exultation in the discovery of the first tastes of limitlessness, were that experience not proceeded by massive doses of the experience of limitation." —Oneness

by Rasha

≋ 6 ≋

Beyond Frustration

THE FACT OF the matter is that a lot of people *do* have trouble manifesting. A number of people are able to just sort of pick up on the process— they read a book or do an exercise and make the magic happen. For many, however, this process is frustrating, elusive and quickly gets chalked up as being "too good to be true." Someone once told me, "New Age rhymes with sewage." I understand this sentiment, in a big way, as I wasn't able to implement the process of manifestation overnight. In fact, it's taken years and years of practice and application to get to this point. More than once in my life I gave up on learning how to manifest and take control of my Reality Creation. I was upset, to say the least. I remember one night when I went on a rampage in my room and tore all my spiritual books on manifestation off the shelf and began stomping on them. What I didn't get at the time was that I was being groomed for a higher purpose. *Why wasn't this damn stuff working anyway?!*

That was when a little voice inside my head, or a feeling, perhaps— I can't even be sure— pointed me back in the direction of things that *did* work. I began to make some connections between the times when things were going well, as opposed to the times when they weren't, and what I happened to be reading or working on during that period. At that moment, I realized that there was a clear distinction between esoteric intangible ideas about spirituality as opposed to practical spiritual techniques that enhanced the quality of life. That was when I realized someone needed to help people understand that it was all about becoming empowered. Needless to say, I accepted the challenge, and I haven't looked back since.

≡ 7 ≡

Who Says You Can't Have What You Want?

WORKING WITH PEOPLE over the years, I have found it helpful to begin the process of manifestation by addressing the reasons why people are unable to create what they want. Oftentimes, understanding how you created your life in the way you have up until this moment can cause spontaneous breakthroughs to occur. Complete changes can happen without even going through the next steps. When you are truly mentally and emotionally clear, you may be able to actually manifest what you want with a mere thought about it. This is why it is important to go through the process of clearing your emotional wounds and mental beliefs. The more you do this, the quicker and easier it will become for you to manifest what you want.

Most people truly do not understand that they are the sole creators of *everything* happening in their lives.

That's why the first step is *always* to get people to see *how* they have been creating what they have so far.

I have found it is usually much easier to manifest a specific event or material item than it is to manifest lasting change in your life. I used to do this; I simply helped people to manifest a specific event or a long-desired material item. It was a lot of fun and rewarding to see the excitement and joy it would bring. However, I began to notice that this one event or item did not bring them the lasting peace or tranquility they deeply desired within their life. After they enjoyed the initial excitement or temporary relief the item or event would bring, it was back to the dreary grindstone that was their life. This is what brought me to the realization that it was more important to help people understand *how* they were creating their lives than to just help them manifest a specific item or event. Sure enough, when I shifted my thinking and began using this new approach, it yielded bigger, more positive and longer-lasting results that were permanently integrated into people's lives.

As an example, one of my clients, an interior decorator that I will refer to as April, was having massive financial difficulties. Throughout our training sessions together, I often spoke to her about how we create our own reality. I explained to her that she was creating financial lack and limitation for herself and that she only needed to turn her thinking around in order to experience greater financial abundance. I gave her an affirmation for magnetizing greater financial opportunities into her life. Low and behold, in a matter of days, April began making more money! However, I noticed that her new-found happiness was short-lived. After about five weeks, she began to appear distraught again. When I asked her how things were going, she told me that they were *okay*. I discovered that April was out of money again, but I felt that something else was at the root of her unhappiness.

What I uncovered was that the problem wasn't her finances at all. Her financial lack was merely a symptom of the greater feeling of lack of love in her life. April was in love with a married man and was also having an affair with him. She would spend a good chunk of every day pining away, wistfully hoping that he would suddenly realize how much he loved her and leave his wife. I explained to her that it was *she* who needed to change her thinking, not *he* who needed to change his lifestyle. I explained that it was up to her to realize she deserved to have her own husband who wanted only to be with her and no one else. After all, the man she was in love with had his cake and was able to eat it too. I asked her the question, "What possible motivation does this man have to change?" From his perspective, right or wrong, he was comfortable because he had it all. He had two women who were fearful enough that they were willing to share one man and pretend like the other woman did not exist.

In the end, April's financial situation was going to stay right where it was because all of her energy was being spent thinking about a married man. In effect, she was draining her energy field and lowering her vibrational rate of attraction. When she finally understood how interconnected her life was and that one area of her life affects all the others, she became motivated to make changes. Once April was able to see how she was creating all of the lack and limitation in her life, she turned it around. After she pulled herself out of her codependent relationship, she was able to give herself back all of the energy she had been pouring into a no-win situation. Her finances righted and she was able to enjoy success in her life again. Today, she is happily married to a faithful man who thinks about no one but her.

In this instance, helping April to manifest more money was not the answer. April needed to become aware of how she was creating her financial lack through the draining process of pouring energy into someone who did not give it back. This became the model by which I began to help people manifest their dream life. *The first step is not to manifest, but to understand how you created your present circumstance. After this step is achieved, the rest is always easy.*

⇛ 8 ⇚

How You Have Created Your Life Thus Far

EVERY PERSON IS already fully creating their own reality in their own way. The difference lies not in becoming a Master, but in the realization that you *are* a Master. I call this self-awareness. In order to effect permanent change in your life, you must become aware of every aspect of yourself. Within your subconscious mind, there exists an aspect referred to as the "unconscious" or "unconscious mind." The unconscious mind is where all of your emotional wounds and limiting beliefs are stored. This is the area of your mind that will work against your best efforts at achieving change until you become aware of what's inside of it. For instance, when it's time to get your bills paid and you suddenly become depressed, it's your unconscious mind. When you snap at people in traffic, it's your unconscious mind. When you spend all of your money and then wonder why you are broke, it's your unconscious mind. When you find yourself in another dead-end relationship that you are scared to let go of, it's your unconscious mind. In other words, any time you do anything at all that causes you struggle or strife, you can bet that it is because of an unconscious mechanism at work in your subconscious mind. When you become aware of and heal what's inside your unconscious mind, you will have success in every area of your life.

≋ 9 ≋

The Unconscious Mind

THE UNCONSCIOUS MIND is part of your mental energy body, which is located within your subconscious mind. The tricky part about your unconscious mind is that you are largely unaware of what is in it. Within your unconscious mind, lie all of your emotional wounds and core beliefs. One reason it is important to begin to understand and clear these areas, is so that you can uncover the hidden motivations behind why you do what you do. If your life is *exactly* the way you want it, chances are you are not holding onto many emotional wounds from the past. However, most people's lives aren't exactly the way they want them to be, and may never be, until they glean the desire to obtain self-awareness. Your stored emotional wounds help create the building blocks and foundation for the way you create your reality. There are many ways in which your emotional wounds will manifest as decisions, choices, and preferences in your daily life. Again, they are un-conscious, which means that you are not aware that they are active. *It is possible to know that you have certain emotional issues, but to still remain unconscious when it comes to enacting the behaviors linked with these issues.*

≋ 10 ≋

Unhealed Emotional Energy

O NE OF MY clients, Janice, showed up for her workout at the gym on time as usual, but I could tell that something wasn't right. She appeared happy and cheery, yet I sensed that inwardly she was sad and depressed. Janice had what I call the "frozen smile" on her face— because her smile was strained and rigid, it looked slightly maniacal. I let it go, however, knowing she would eventually want to talk about it. Sure enough, halfway through the workout, she said, "You know, I could die and nobody would even know." She polished her statement off with a forced hardy laugh. In this instance, Janice was not redirecting her reality with positive thoughts, she was instead repressing her emotional energy.

Janice was always very vivacious; I had noticed earlier that no less than four younger guys said hello to her on the way into the gym. So I waited, knowing that the right time would present itself to approach her on this issue. At the end of the workout, right before we left, I pointed out the fact that I had observed the young men talking to her when she walked in. Janice pointedly told me that I was full of it, but as I predicted, she was again accosted by the same four young men on the way out. Once we got outside the door, Janice turned to me, rolling her eyes, and said reluctantly, "Okay, you got me, what do I do?" She knew from listening to me that I would never let anyone wallow in their problems, there was always a solution. At this point, she was ready to listen to what I had to say because she knew I was onto her self-pity.

Oftentimes in these situations, I will have some sort of sudden insight into other people's lives and the right words just seem to come to me. So I told her in no uncertain terms that she would be contacted by someone special who would let her know how much she meant to them. She was elated, excited, and curious, all at the same time, because she had seen me at work before and knew that I had a way of making things happen. It is really as simple as thinking about the most positive thing that could happen in someone's life and then helping them to allow it to happen. I do this by building a belief system in my own ability to do it first. After that, it is easier to influence other people's beliefs, as well. Once I have influenced someone's belief system, I can help them to create what they want in their life. So she said, "Okay, you're on!"

Three days later, Janice came in for her second session of the week. She could barely contain herself and said, "I cannot believe it, you were right!" As this was far from the first time I had affected somebody's Reality Creation with a positive belief, I was not the slightest bit surprised. However, I am always excited to hear about what happened. Janice told me, "My first true love contacted me via email after seven years of not hearing from him!" She went on to say that he wrote he was unhappily married and thought about her all the time. Janice was so excited, that whatever happened next hardly mattered. The most important thing, really, was that she knew she was never truly abandoned by anyone except herself. All she had to do was release her self-pity, get excited, and start focusing on what she really wanted in her life. Her unhealed emotional energy of abandonment had resurfaced and begun to affect her Reality Creation.

In fact, this energy can affect you so much so that you will not be able to observe any evidence to the contrary. You will only see what your emotional wounds say are real. You will not see all the love that is there for you until you allow yourself to do so.

Unhealed emotional energy is actually carried within the body, or bio-energetic sphere. This emotional baggage serves to wreak havoc on our entire energy system; the results can be seen both in our physical body and in our Reality Creation. The origin of this energy can have many different sources, but it can always be traced back to either emotional trauma or environmental absorption. It has also now been proven that you can pick up this energy at any time, even while you're in infancy. One theory, now supported by some psychologists and hypnotherapists, is that before we are born we have chosen some of the painful events and circumstances in our lives to become more powerful or empowered. According to this theory, we even chose our parents to help us learn these life lessons. If this is true, then we are truly creating every single thing in our lives and just waking up to our unlimited potential.

≥ 11 ≤

Emotional Trauma

W HEN AN EVENT that creates an extreme emotional reaction happens to you at an early age, it generally becomes life-altering. This is because you tend to make decisions in the moment or immediately after an emotionally traumatic event occurs. Your decision is based upon the need to make sure that this never happens to you again. Thus, you subconsciously form an energy body based on this decision, or what some psychologists and spiritual teachers refer to as a *sub-personality*. The job of the sub-personality is to assure you that you will never have to go through this particular painful event ever again. In other words, the sub-personality is there to protect you. It takes on an energy of its own, derived from your personal power source, and subconsciously motivates you to make certain choices and decisions that will keep you out of harm's way. This is all well and good during that particular moment or time period in your life, because at that point it was a needed survival mechanism. However, sub-personalities are fear-based and drain your energy in the attempt to keep you from re-experiencing the emotional wounds of the past. What's tricky is learning to recognize that you are *presently* creating a reality based upon the fears of a sub-personality that was formed in the *past*. A sub-personality may have been protecting you for so long that you mistakenly perceive it as *who you are*. But, it is not who you are; *it is who you were*.

The sub-personality not only acts as a protector, it often takes over your persona entirely. When you look back upon the events of your life, you may give credit to some of the bad things that you experienced because you feel like they made you *stronger*. This is generally a healthy practice because you are turning a negative into a positive. You may also have attained the heightened level of understanding that everything in your life happens for your personal growth and development. The problem arises when you strongly identify with the emotional wound. Holding onto the wound because *it makes you who you are* will hinder your ability to create the life you want. Further, it bolsters the strength of the particular sub-personality associated with that wound or event, and strengthens the constrictive parameters of the reality that sub-personality creates for you.

I have seen many cases where a sub-personality becomes someone's "assumed" identity. As a general rule, the person is unaware that this has taken place.

A sub-personality can make a person sullen and with-drawn, or perhaps it makes them outgoing and gregari-ous. There is nothing wrong with either of these qualities, as long as the person is *consciously* choosing one of them. But most people aren't consciously creating their realities. Unfortunately, most people, to one degree or another, are creating their life from the fear-based perspective of an unhealed part of themselves that has become a sub-personality.

This is where what has served you in the past quite well can eventually become outdated and turn into a prison. You emotional wounds may have actually pushed you towards achievements or success, until one day you to realize that you aren't really where you want to be. Perhaps you were motivated by your *invalidated child* sub-personality, which is always trying to get peo-ple's attention. The problem with this is that, no matter how much attention or recognition you get, it will never be enough. This is because you are not really creating what *you want*—you are creating what your *emotional wound wants*.

Perhaps you are having trouble amassing any amount of wealth or seeing things through to completion. Here, you could be seeing the results of issues you have about deserving or being worthy of having the good you want in your life; issues based on the belief that you are not good enough to have or achieve certain things. This sub-personality or emotional wound may have been formed from being told that you were not good enough or from being born into a family that didn't think that *they* were good enough. In either case, you will not be happy because you are not creating what you really want. Again, you are creating what your emotional wound wants. *In essence, you can become trapped within the confines of your emotional wounds, continuously creating and recreating the same reality over and over again.*

Emotional trauma can be slight or it can be severe. It can result from being a rape victim or from being a child who was ignored. In either case, your reality creation can be affected. Do not underestimate the power that an event could have on your ability to consciously create your reality. *Oftentimes, individuals may think they have done all the work they need to do on a certain issue; that they have moved on. If you are having trouble creating exactly what you want, the work is not done.*

≋ 12 ≋

Environmental Absorption

RESEARCH NOW SHOWS us that you can be affected unconsciously even during the brief stay in your mother's womb. You are emotionally and energetically vulnerable from the time right before birth and throughout most of your childhood. The emotional status of your mother, along with the environment she was surrounded by, will become logged into your subconscious and manifest as certain behavioral patterns. This is why some expectant mothers take the time out to play music for their unborn child, because inherently they know they can affect their child's development even before birth. It may be hard to believe, but you can have unconscious emotional responses running from even before you were born.

Your childhood ends up being the primary source of most of your emotional baggage and unconscious behavioral patterns. Here is where you make key life decisions, and formulate your beliefs and behavioral patterns around those decisions. If your parents were always scrimping and scraping to make enough money to pay the bills or for food, you may find yourself obsessed with making money as you get older. You may have made the decision that you were never going to be in that situation again. To a certain degree, this idea can serve to motivate you to create wealth in your life. However, you are now creating wealth from a fear-based perspective. You are not creating for the joy of being wealthy; you are creating out of the fear of winding up back in that place with your parents. In this case, you will never be truly happy because you are not creating what you want; you are trying to avoid what you don't want.

Another way to form a belief is to be told that you are not worthy or deserving of something. You may have been told that you will not amount to anything or that you are not going to be able to achieve the things you wish to achieve. Or, you may have been told that you need to be "realistic." Perhaps you have developed the belief that *you are not worthy of love or that love must be earned.* This can occur simply from having an aloof parent who ignored you. The resultant feeling is that if love is freely given, then there must be something wrong with it. This unconscious belief could manifest in your intimate relationship. Since you had to work hard to get your parents' attention through all manner of unhealthy behaviors and stimuli, you now work hard to get your mate's attention, as well. Then, after all kinds of hard work intended to get and capture your mate's attention, when they really open up to you, you become scared or aloof. You will then sabotage this relationship because your unconscious belief is that true love is never freely given. Emotionally, you are an ignored five-year old in an adult body trying to win someone's attention because you feel unloved and powerless. Two people together in this type of relationship may unconsciously battle for power and control, taking turns feeling powerful and powerless.

Hearing your parents or other people argue about things can also formulate issues for you that will manifest later on in your life. You listen to key themes being hashed out, generally in unhealthy ways, and then make decisions as a child that are acted out physically as an adult. This is from the environmental energy that you absorbed during those time periods. Thus, in this example, you absorb the energy of *resolution through egoic clashes* between parental figures. Later on in life, you may find yourself creating situations that seem to call out for an argument to settle something. You could even say with a degree of accuracy that you have become magnetic to a life partner who also likes to settle things through arguing. But be honest with yourself, who really wants to argue all the time? Continued arguing or conflict with your mate serves to lower your vibrational field and compromise your ability to consciously and purposefully create your reality.

≋ 13 ≋

The Rocky Road

IN FACT, IT is *because of* the many challenges I've hurdled and the varied life experiences I've had, that I became interested in the field of human development. For the life of me, I just couldn't understand why success in not just one, but virtually every area of my life was elusive. I struggled and strained against the currents of life until I finally began the path of internal study and self-awareness. If I had not worked through many obstacles myself, and encountered the life lessons I needed to master, I would not be able to understand what people go through. Knowledge is wholly insufficient when it comes to teaching human development. Wisdom is *applied knowledge,* and the only way you can get that is from having worked through your own life lessons. How can you help somebody without first having learned to help yourself?

Here I have labeled some of the forms of consciousness that people enact. They are actually forms of unconscious behavior that take on an aspect of your consciousness and become the way you create your reality. Thus, they are labeled as forms of consciousness, even though they represent unconsciousness. There are many different forms of unconscious behavior, but I have included a few of the key forms of this behavior that I have personally worked through.

≣ 14 ≣

Poverty Consciousness

A CLASSIC EXAMPLE of unconscious behavior is the inability to save money while making the best efforts at attempting to do so. One way you can see this behavior manifesting is when you find yourself *spending as much as you're earning.* You may even get a new job with better pay so that you can finally begin to save money. However, because you unconsciously do not believe you deserve to have money or perhaps unconsciously associate having money with some sort of fear from your past, you begin spending more to compensate. Magically, your spending has increased with your earning and you still have no money left over to save. This behavior can stem from a simple lack of discipline, or it can be from feeling you are not deserving and worthy of having a lot of money.

Growing up in my family, whenever you had money, you spent it. Very simple. As soon as the welfare check came in or payday rolled around (depending upon the time period of my childhood), it was time to celebrate! My mom would go out, buy a whole bunch of groceries and sweets, and we would feast. My dad would take us to Taco Bell. But, whether I was staying with my mom or my dad, the feeling was one of happiness when money came in. Then, when the money was gone, it was back to poverty and the negative emotions that would result from it. Thus, money was viewed by me as something special and extraordinary that was fleeting. It was there as a reward only, not as a regular way of life. This formula developed in my subconscious as an unconscious behavioral pattern.

It wasn't until I was 30 that I began to uncover this particular pattern of behavior and managed to save some money. When I first learned how to manifest things, in my late 20's, and began to manifest bigger financial opportunities, I still had no money. I still felt helpless and depressed because I never seemed to be able to accumulate any amount of money. My life continued to be a series of highs and lows. In this way, I began to understand the need for self-awareness and taking responsibility for creating my life.

After I attained enough awareness to observe myself in action, I was able to make the connection between my present-day adult behavior and my childhood environment. *I had been repeating the same pattern as my parents of making money and then spending it as quickly as I could. Getting better paying jobs was just like putting a bigger motor on the same old rickety boat with holes in it, I was getting nowhere even faster.* However, becoming aware of my unconscious behavior was like finally deciding to fix the boat and plug up the holes. Sudden awareness of self, in and of itself, can cause you to spontaneously heal and correct unconscious behavioral patterns. Shortly afterward, I began to save money and was able to enjoy having more abundance in my life.

≋ 15 ≋

Judgment Consciousness

I FOUND OUT that a super great way to keep all the best things from popping up in my own life was to judge other people for having or getting them. I'm not even sure where this judgment came from. All I know is that, from as early as I can remember, I judged all the kids who had more than I did. I was never truly grateful for the efforts of my parents while they struggled and toiled with their own poverty consciousness. I just knew that other kids *had* and I *had not*. This became an unfortunate foundation for my Reality Creation later as a young adult.

If you know anything about judgment, then you know it is an emotion that has an extremely low vibrational frequency. When you see someone who is doing something or has something you want to experience, and then judge them for it, you are assuring that you will never get to experience it. In other words, you are creating a lower vibrational energy field while in the process of observing something that you want. You may be feeling that this person is bad because they have what you have always wanted, or that they are bad because *only bad people have good things*. However, your subconscious mind registers this feeling as indicating that *having the good things you want means you're a bad person*.

You cannot and will not become wealthy by judging wealthy people for having wealth. As a matter of fact, you will push wealthy people away from you by consciously or unconsciously judging them. You will also push the idea of wealth away from you. You cannot get a healthy lean body by judging healthy lean people. You won't attract your dream partner by judging people who have amazing relationships. You will not achieve your dream life by judging people who are living the life of their dreams. In other words, you cannot have anything that you judge someone else for having, period. It will never come to you until you release your judgment about it. If you have a judgment about *anything at all*, you have work to do.

The only good judgment is what I refer to as "natural judgment," or the ability to discern what is or is not for your own highest good. You achieve this by paying attention to your *feeling power*. You were born with the wonderful innate gift of always knowing what is in your best interest. The problem is that people often outthink themselves. Your feeling power will provide you with a better guidance system than your logical thinking brain, every time, on time. You may be attached to how smart you think you are. You may have studied extensively in one field or another and accumulated a vast body of knowledge. However, you may have also bolstered your own ego to the point of shutting yourself off from your intuitive feeling power, which always knows better than you do. In turn, this impairs your ability to make natural judgments. When you begin to clear yourself and spend some time in meditation, you will also begin to get back in touch with this inborn natural resource.

At any moment in time, you have access to your feeling power. Your feeling power does not stem from your intellectual awareness, it stems from your heart center. Many people refer to it as your 'gut instinct,' although this is still incorrect. A feeling in your gut is actually fear-based, whereas a feeling that comes from your heart center will indicate whether or not something is actually for your highest good. If you are about to interview for a job, buy a house or get a new apartment, go out on a first date with a potential life partner, or make a huge financial decision, your feeling power can guide you in the right direction. Because at a deeper level you have an innate knowingness that will guide you, you can always make guided decisions in life. If you get quiet with yourself before and/or during the process of making these big decisions, you will get a feeling about it. It is the first thing that you feel, before your intellect kicks in and starts weighing the pros and cons. This is why meditation is a great way to enhance this ability, because it quiets down a lot of the mental chatter that only get's in the way of making good decisions.

The flip side of the coin is judging things that you do not like or want in your experience. It's true that a lot of people trick themselves into thinking they don't want what they believe they can't have. However, most people are aware of what they really don't want. The problem comes when you become judgmental about what you don't want. The difference between a negative, egoic judgment, as opposed to natural judgment, is that in natural judgment there is no negative emotional charge involved, meaning that you do not have strong negative feelings about it. A choice pops up and it simply feels good or it doesn't. No problem, you choose based upon the feeling that you get about it and continue on. If you are honest with yourself about how it feels, your choice will be always be rewarding. When you are being *judgmental*, or egoically judging something based upon your unconscious beliefs about it, you will be projecting a negative emotional charge on it. When you do this, you are actually magnetizing it into your life and drawing this unwanted thing right to you. You needn't fear your thoughts, however. You need only pay attention to what you have an emotional charge to. It's when you have a strong negative or positive emotional charge to something that you actually become magnetic to it. Thus, it is important to understand judgment consciousness, as it is a great way to discern how you may be unconsciously drawing certain people, places, and situations into your life that you do not want. You can easily know that something or someone is not for your highest good without having to judge it as bad. In fact, there is no good or bad. Again, it is only what is for your highest good and what is not.

It is important to remember that everything exists at a certain vibrational frequency. Since all of the things you want to experience exist at a higher frequency—like abundance of money, healthy body, and a happy relationship—judgment will not bring them into your life. Instead, you will get the people, places, and circumstances that vibrationally resonate with your current emotional state of judgment. Perhaps you see someone in line at the grocery store who is wearing something you find offensive or acting in a manner that you find disruptive. Instead of ignoring them, you find yourself harshly judging them. The more you focus upon them and the more emotionally charged your judgment about them becomes, the more likely you are to draw their attention to you. Don't be surprised if they glare at you angrily or walk up to you and say something.

Conversely, the more excited and enthusiastic about something you are, the quicker you will bring it to you. If you were standing in line at the grocery store behind somebody you really admired or were extremely attracted to, you could wind up drawing them right to you, as well. You might find them extremely interesting, or perhaps you are attracted to them. The more you feel this way, the greater the emotional charge, the more likely you are to draw them to you. Of course, this particular example is not to be confused with lusting over someone, which is a lower vibration than joy and happiness, and could actually repel them away from you.

Judgment is usually a projection coming from a part of you that is *fearful* of having or experiencing what another person has or gets to experience. During one of the more negative periods in my life, I had become very cynical. I was extremely judgmental of the world and the people in it. It was coincidentally during a time period when I also felt very helpless and powerless. The more trapped in my own vicious cycle I became, the more I judged other people around me. I judged the people who had what I wanted for having it, and I judged the people I felt were bad for getting away with living their lives the way they were. In other words, I judged people for having what I wanted and judged people for having what I didn't want. Talk about a no-win situation! The answer came to me one day that my judgment needed to come to an end. I was sitting at the coffee shop, surrounded by people who were all having a great time. Someone parking their car in the lot had their stereo cranked on high, bassing the entire shopping complex. I was extremely irritated and immediately looked around for validation to see if other people were irritated as well. To my amazing surprise, no one else seemed to be the slightest bit bothered by this event. They were all still smiles and laughter, having a great time, completely oblivious to my extreme discomfort at the loud music. On top of that, there were other people in the coffee shop who were peacefully reading their books, completely unbothered by the music. It suddenly clicked in, at a deeper level in my conscious awareness, that everybody else was too busy creating what they wanted in life to be bothered by what anybody else was doing. Holy cow! I was so busy judging all the people around me for this, that, and the other thing, that none of my energy had been directed towards what I wanted. In essence, all of my attention was being directed towards what I didn't want. I then realized that I could never magnetize anything I wanted into my life as long as I stayed in judgment consciousness.

In a flash of inspiration, I got out a piece of paper and began writing down all the people in the world I judged for having what they had and for what I felt like they were getting away with. When I was done, I had a very large list; it included rap stars, political figures, athletes, financial geniuses, drug dealers, celebrities, millionaires, homeless people, and everyone in between. My own fear of success, combined with my cynical attitude about the world, was creating massive amounts of judgment wherever I went. Ironically, I was also scared to leave the house, because my strong negativity was continuously magnetizing negative circumstances into my life. After I created this huge list, I rewrote it with the phrase "is good" at the end of each item on the list. I had specific names, as well as generalities, all of which now ended with "is good" or even "is great."

That night I had an amazing dream: The dream took place in the basement of a warehouse. In this place, from behind shelves and stacks of boxes and from every possible corner you can imagine, came a whole slew of assassins. They used every sort of medieval weapon you could think of to try and get me, but I was invincible.

I used kicks, punches, ducked, swung, flipped, you name it. I took all of them out with amazing accuracy and didn't get a scratch on me! I woke up the next morning feeling really great, revitalized and refreshed; much more positive than I had in a long time. It was then that my dream came back to me and I realized I had defeated all of the judgments in my unconscious basement.

Releasing Judgment

- First, realize that anytime you hold a negative feeling about anything you are only lowering your own vibrational rate of attraction.
- Next, take out a piece of paper and write down a list of every single person that you have a judgment about. It doesn't matter how justified you feel or how much you can rationalize it, judging something is still only focusing your energy on what you don't want.
- Next, I dare you to actually write down the words "is good" or even "is great!" at the end of each name or description that you come up with. If you want emotional freedom, then this step is necessary. Remember, you need emotional freedom to master your reality creation.
- After you are done, then let it go. The very act of doing this will free up energy in your bio-energetic sphere and elevate your vibrational rate of attraction. Don't be surprised either, if you have a symbolic dream about it, representing more freedom and power in your life.

◆ What if every single person in the world gave up their judgments about all the other people in the world? Remember, the only reason you don't want to give up your judgments is because you are scared that someone else won't give up their judgments about you.

≡ 16 ≡

Externalization Consciousness

MY NEXT ACHIEVEMENT in self-awareness was in the area of relationships. From very early on, I seemed to gravitate towards women who had a tendency to want to control me. I bounced from relationship to relationship, not understanding how I was continuously recreating the exact same relationship over and over again. *Why did these women always want to control me?* I couldn't understand it. What I didn't realize at the time was *that was what I wanted*; I wanted someone to take over for me and play mommy. There were only too many women ready and willing to play that role for me. For every person willing to role-play codependency, there will always be a partner willing to play along with you. The Universe is abundant in everything you desire, unconsciously as well as consciously.

The first step for me in breaking this cycle was becoming aware that I was continuously magnetizing women into my life who exemplified this type of partner; each one was even more extreme than the woman before her. Eventually, I reached the point where I was tired of the lesson. Sometimes you just have to learn the hard way. I discovered that this was true for me, as well as for many of the people I've worked with. The very last person in my life who exemplified this behavioral pattern was a woman who became very abusive. After I extracted myself from that relationship, I vowed I would never recreate a situation like that for myself again. From there, I began to explore why I was creating this pattern and what lesson I needed to learn. The lesson turned out to be about power and what it feels like to externalize your power, or give it away.

The unfortunate thing about this type of lesson is that it cannot be taught, it can only be experienced. You can teach awareness around it, but you cannot teach someone to quit giving their power away in relationships. This is why I write extensively about power and power in relationships, not only does it make up a major portion of your vibrational field, but is also one of the most difficult areas of your life to glean awareness. However, oftentimes through the reading of real life examples and lessons learned, some spontaneous awareness can be integrated into one's consciousness.

The first thing I noticed after I made the decision to stop externalizing my power in relationships was that I became more successful. It caused me to take more responsibility for myself and cultivate more internal power, as well. I had more energy, felt more upbeat, and had more success. Then, on top of everything else, I began magnetizing to myself a new kind of partner. I began to have relationships that were more loving, less codependent, and more respectful of each other. In this new type of relationship I was neither needy nor needed, only a mutual wanting. In essence, my new mate would be an outer reflection of my new inner feeling of self-respect and empowerment.

Most often, externalizing your power comes from not having any sense of self. One of my life lessons was to develop and cultivate an inner sense of self, to provide meaning for myself. My search was always directed outwardly; I was always looking outside of myself instead of within. I constantly sought out the advice of anyone who I perceived *had it together* or was an authority of some sort. I became a leaf blowing in the wind; each new person I encountered would send me blowing in a different direction. I would give my power to this person and then that person, trying to figure out what I should do with my life. The answer was always different every time.

I finally had to realize that no one else outside of myself could provide me with what I was looking for. I had to be the one to give myself what I needed. I did that by realizing that I was deserving and worthy of being on this planet. I realized that we are all here to create what we want; we only have to make sure that we harm no one else in the process of creating what we want. After I really understood this concept, I also intuitively began to understand how limited my thinking had been. In essence, I had become wrapped up in the process of trying to become someone I am not. You are perfect just the way you are. When you stop and realize that you have the power to create your own reality, you will never externalize your power ever again.

≋ 17 ≋

Victim Consciousness

L EARNING ABOUT VICTIM consciousness was one of the greatest things that ever happened to me. I used to get mad at everything. I would get mad at the traffic, mad at the parking meter maid, mad at my job, mad at my girlfriend, mad at my body—mad at the world. It was always someone or something else's fault, never mine. When something didn't go the way I wanted, out came the *pointer finger* to find a reason for it. Mysteriously, the finger never seemed to point at me, it always pointed outwards away from me. The reason the finger never found me was because I was unconsciously acting out the victim and victims never point fingers at themselves.

The beginning of victim consciousness starts with the question, "Why me?" This unfortunate question became the validation for perpetuating my own worst nightmares. It's also a great excuse to do nothing about something. I was always able to find plenty of reasons in life why I couldn't do what I said I wanted to do. If someone else had achieved the goal or dream I desired, I felt it was because they were lucky or born into it. The problem with that theory revealed itself when I finally began to meet some of the people I had previously assumed were born into success or just lucky. A few *were* actually born into success and had enjoyed great advantages early on in life. However, the majority of these big achievers started from even more humble beginnings than myself, and had endured even more arduous trials than I had.

They all had one thing in common that stuck with me; they never blamed anyone for anything. Never. Period. One time, a personal friend of mine who was one of these great achievers, began making suggestions to me about a multi-million dollar company that I could run myself, even offering to help me get started. I promptly replied that I didn't know how, it would be too stressful and it would tie up all my time. He paused for a moment, looked at me and said, "It's actually pretty easy." This particular individual was a Mexican immigrant, raised by a single mother with an alcoholic father, and *he* was telling *me* how easy it was?! His secret to success? He was never a victim, nothing ever *happened* to him. Instead, *he* happened to life. As a result, he was one of the most successful people I knew, with five successful businesses and a dozen investment properties. The idea that anything outside of him was in control of his life never, ever entered his mind.

When I began taking responsibility for my choices and all the negative energy I had been creating, my life made a turn to the positive. As soon as I quit complaining, I started to actually make forward progress in my life. You see, when you stop complaining, you actually have a chance to listen. And, when you listen, you learn. I began to see how I was the creator of it all. I was the one that parked without paying attention to where the red lines were. I was the one that decided to drive at 8:30 am in the morning when traffic is heaviest. I was the one that stayed up late the night before so that I wasn't well rested and thinking as clearly as I should. I was the one who kept showing up each day to a job I did not love. I was the one who previously chose to seek out my mates in the confines of bars and under the influence of alcohol. I was the one who couldn't balance my checkbook. I was the one who chose not to take vacations. There was no one else telling me to do these things, these were decisions that I made. I cannot tell you how powerful I became when I decided to quit complaining about the people, places, and circumstances that I put myself in and around.

≡ 18 ≡

Powerlessness Consciousness

A LTHOUGH I WAS now reaping some of the benefits from mastering many of my wonderful life lessons, I still had one big lesson left to learn. As it turned out, there was an underlying theme to most of my other life lessons, as well. Just like peeling back the layers of an onion, I began to get to the core of me and see a larger picture. By far, my largest life lesson was recognizing that the root of my problems stemmed from my constant attention-seeking behavior and my unquenchable need for outside validation. In one form or another, I had spent my entire life trying to impress people or to become the center of attention.

I acted out this behavior in some seriously unhealthy ways. In my pursuit of becoming the center of attention, I would put myself in situations that became destructive to my life and my health. For awhile, in order to achieve a bigger, better-looking body that would get more attention, I experimented with steroids. This led to taking other drugs, getting a DUI, and jail on three separate occasions. It's amazing what you'll do when you want to impress someone. Ultimately, this is the most disempowering place to be. That was where I lived for many years, inside of an empty shell, always looking for someone or something to give me meaning.

The problem was that I was always looking outside of myself for definition. Who was I? I had no idea who I was. Another problem with this was that I was scared all the time. I was always scared; both consciously of confrontation, as well as unconsciously that someone would find out that I had no sense of self-worth. This manifested when other guys in the gym or at clubs would look at me funny or start something with me. Oftentimes, I would be the one doing the funny looking at other guys, out of fear that they were looking at me. But, whenever someone actually called me out on it, I almost always backed down. The reason? There was nothing inside of me worth defending. Because I didn't have a good enough reason to defend myself, I couldn't muster the strength to stand up for myself. It was a vicious cycle, but an invaluable learning tool for me.

I learned that other people cannot give me meaning or determine my destiny. I learned that I must cultivate my own feeling of self-worth and the inner strength of being that nobody else could provide. It was not until I gained this basic understanding and awareness that my first genuine life teachers showed up. I had to want it, though, and be willing to commit to it, before I could become magnetic to the teachers that would help me cultivate my own inner sense of self. In the end, even they could not give me this meaning; they were only there to show me the way.

I am thankful and grateful for all the life lessons I was gifted with in this lifetime. If it weren't for these wonderful lessons, I could not be writing this book and doing my part in the elevation of consciousness on Earth. I came to the conclusion that there were only "life lessons," not "problems or mistakes." Once you realize this concept for yourself, you will become unstoppable in the pursuit of your dreams.

≋ 19 ≋

Cultivating an Inner Sense of Power

I'VE DEFINED POWER as the ability to provide yourself with options for manifesting the things that are important to you in your life. Power can mean many different things to different people. For some it can mean financial prosperity, while for others it can mean physical health. It can mean your ability to create a healthy relationship with a mate, or your ability to help people in need. It all boils down to how effective you feel in the world.

For many years I relied upon my physical body as my sense of power. When I developed a tear in my rotator cuff, my world turned upside down. My body no longer functioned as it used to and I lost close to 25 lbs of muscle inside of two years. I struggled with simple tasks, like opening and closing the car door, as well as carrying groceries with my left arm. It did, however, provide me with the opportunity to cultivate an inner sense of power; an ability I have found to be invaluable as I've learned to master my Reality Creation.

Even though I had developed an imposing physical body, I still never felt truly powerful. I had fooled myself into believing I was powerful, yet I remained very fearful inside. Thus, I had never cultivated the inner sense of power that would give me the faith to create *whatever* I wanted for myself. Ironically, the injury to my shoulder was the catalyst that would drive me to discover the foundation for true power in my life. What the next five years would bring, I could not, and would not fathom, as I struggled against my own body's resistance to healing itself. The further irony was that I was a specialist in rehabilitation and had helped many people to recover from various injuries.

One day someone said to me, "Do you think that your shoulder is trying to tell you something?" Indeed it had been; my shoulder was telling me that I did not feel powerful. Try as I may, I could not heal it. *What I found out was that I needed to release my fear— fear of abandonment, fear of helplessness. My ultimate fear was that no matter what, somebody could always come along and do whatever they wanted to me.* That no matter how hard I tried, I could not escape the feeling that at some level I was powerless to the outside world. It was thus that the answers began to come, slowly. Upon the realization of what was truly happening inside of me, I was able to refocus my efforts from my physical body to my spiritual body. Thus I began in earnest to build a spiritual foundation of faith in something greater than myself, as I strengthened faith in my ability to tap into this power, and faith that I was a worthy of being on the planet.

Once I began releasing my fear, my shoulder began to heal. Very slowly, mind you, but the healing process had finally begun. Happily, the more I focused upon releasing fear and helplessness, the more powerful I felt and the healthier my body became. To do this, I utilized the emotional release techniques you will find later in this book.

≋ 20 ≋

The Two Ways You Act Out
Unconscious Behavior

THERE ARE TWO basic ways of perpetuating unconscious behavior in our lives. The first one I call **active unconscious behavior**. Active unconscious behavior means that *you are unaware of how you create your reality*. This type of unconscious behavior usually constitutes the larger portion of your growth and development as you struggle to hurdle the obstacles that you are unknowingly putting in your own path. You cannot successfully create your own reality and remain in this type of consciousness at the same time. All of my great life lessons, some of which I've mentioned and many that I did not, occurred as a result of my living in this type of consciousness.

When you are living your life in active unconscious behavior, you literally have no idea why your life is the way it is. You do not understand why you keep getting into the same relationships over and over again. You do not understand why you cannot get a better job. You don't get where all the extra pounds of weight are coming from. You cannot comprehend the idea that it is YOU who are creating all of it. In order for most people to get past their active unconscious behavior, they have to have a burning desire to do, be, or experience more of what life has to offer. Either they have finally become fed up with their situation, or they just finally realize that they truly want more. Until they reach a point of real urgency, they will not be motivated— nor will they have the energy— to learn, do and apply all that is necessary to elevate themselves out of this level of thinking and being. This is not a judgment; there is no right or wrong. We are where we are and it does not benefit anyone when we judge ourselves or another on the path. However, coming to the sudden realization that you have been living your life unconsciously is a great achievement. One of the most important goals of this book, in fact, is to help you come to this realization.

The other way you act out unconscious behavior is what I, and many others, refer to, as **reactive unconscious behavior**. This is a more easily recognizable and correctible form of unconscious behavior. Correcting this type of behavior can also help you to manifest greater things for yourself in life. When you are operating in reactive unconscious behavior, you will react to any stimulus that triggers your emotional instability. You will react to traffic, a fellow employee at work who annoys you, somebody who bumps into you in the store, a bill in the mail, a parking ticket, your spouse or mate, your children—anything at all that stimulates you.

When viewed through this type of unconscious behavior, life happens to you, not the other way around. Everything seems to be coming at you all the time, almost as if the world is out to get you. You bump into the wall or door and suddenly it is as if the wall or door attacked you. Your children are not behaving the way they are supposed to, never mind the fact that they are *children* and prone to act that way. You become irritable, angry, and defensive, trying to defend yourself against an aggressive world. In his book *Soul Sword: The Way and Mind of a Zen Warrior*, Vernon Kitabu Tuner refers to this type of behavior as "push button" consciousness. Basically, you walk around all day with a big red button sticking out that says "push me for a reaction." In severe circumstances, you become completely helpless to your big red button and bounce around from situation to situation, feeling more and more negatively.

You must elevate yourself beyond this way of daily living if you wish to be in command of your reality creation and manifest your dreams. Think about it for a second, what chance do you have of purposefully creating the life of your dreams if you are constantly yelling at your wife, husband, or your kids? Zero. What chance do you have of purposefully directing your thoughts towards a beautiful vacation on an island paradise if you are always cussing someone out in traffic? Not much. How will you get into the "feeling place" of having your dream home in the mountains if you are angry at work all of the time? Good luck. When you begin to meditate, you will create the space in your life to *act* instead of *react*. This is a good starting place towards diminishing your reactive unconscious behavior and taking command of your reality creation.

Diminishing Reactive Unconscious Behavior
- When you wake up in the morning, take a moment to sit in silence.
- When you get into your car, take three deep breathes before you start the engine.
- When you get to work, take three deep breathes before you start your day.
- On your lunch break, sit still and close your eyes for five minutes.

≋ 21 ≋

Your Beliefs Create Your Reality

W HEN I LIVED in Los Angeles, I used to hit the Starbucks bordering West L.A. and Brentwood every morning before work. There was this homeless guy, Lyle, who would chat me up every day. From the first time I met Lyle, I knew there was something different about him. Lyle always seemed much more positive and upbeat than your average homeless guy on the street. As a result of this, I enjoyed interacting with him, as well as giving him occasional money and free coffees. Because I never, ever quit talking about the power of manifestation and the ability to create what you want, Lyle began to visibly look forward to our daily morning meetings. We carried on this way for about three months straight, me going on and on about manifestation, him intently listening.

One day, Lyle decided it was time to share a secret with me. Lyle walked with a limp and I had always assumed that he was either born that way or just had some really, really bad luck. I mean, Good Lord, he was already homeless *and* he had to have a limp, too?! So, Lyle pulled me aside and said, "You know man, this limp ain't real." He then preceded, much out of sight of the regular clientele at Starbucks, to walk back and forth perfectly normally. I laughed out loud for no less than 15 minutes! He *had* me. Lyle then got to the point of this whole demo and said, "You know, I never really believed that I could do much of anything. But, after talking and listening to you for the last three months, I really am starting to believe that I *can* do whatever I want!" Lyle told me that after my last talk with him about creating what you want, he decided that he was going to go home to New Orleans to find an old buddy who had wanted to start up a business with him back in the day. The key here was that I could see how Lyle now *believed* he could do whatever he wanted. He told me he was going to pack up his stuff at the shelter and take a bus to New Orleans. The last thing he said to me was, "Man, I just want your phone number because one day I want to be able to tell you that I made it."

Sure enough, the next day I came for my regular tall peppermint mocha-no whip and Lyle was gone. I never saw or heard from him again for an entire year. Then one day, just as I was getting ready to leave L.A. for good, I received a phone call out of the blue. It was Lyle. He told me that he had a business selling books and that he and his partner were earning over $200,000 a year! Holy mother of pearl! I was elated. This was more than any reward anyone could ever have given me; it provided me with a sense of accomplishment and added purpose to my own life. THAT was the reward!

If you wish to purposefully create and manifest your reality, it is vital that you become aware of your beliefs and begin to understand how they affect your life. Without question, you create your reality within the parameters of your beliefs. You have beliefs about yourself and beliefs about the world— beliefs about how good the world is, as well as beliefs about how unfair it is. You have beliefs about how well you do some things and about how badly you do others. You carry beliefs that you are consciously aware of, as well as unconscious beliefs from early childhood that you have no awareness of whatsoever.

Most people have a mass of conflicting beliefs, conscious and unconscious, that they struggle and strain against. This, in turn, creates emotional highs and lows that hinder their ability to manifest what they want. As an example, for a long time in my life I struggled with two conflicting beliefs that were running in my consciousness. I had the belief that I was a *go-getter who could generate a lot of money*. This was a conscious belief of which I was aware; I also happened to like this trait in myself. At the same time, I had an unconscious belief that I was *not worthy or deserving of having money*. In other words, when I finally did start making more money, I would just as quickly spend it and thus stay broke. In this case, I had two beliefs, one conscious and one unconscious, that were literally working against each other. I wasted tremendous amounts of my energy trying to physically rectify this situation by looking for more ways to make money. In the end, I finally became aware of the fact that I was unconsciously sabotaging myself via my hidden beliefs about how I wasn't worthy and deserving. I had to address the unconscious beliefs I had about myself if I was ever going to amass any kind of wealth whatsoever. I further realized that I could become a millionaire and it wouldn't matter. Until I released these limiting beliefs about myself, I would spend or find some way to lose all the money I was making in order to keep myself at the place where I was subconsciously comfortable.

In fact, this is something that can happen to you when you begin to master your reality creation. You can literally allow yourself to experience people, places, and situations in life that would have made you previously uncomfortable. You may open yourself up to experiences that you would have never dared to before, spontaneously even, that are now magically within your grasp. You may even find that you now feel free to want and experience more. You may even dare to expand on your list of wants when you have less limiting beliefs holding you back.

Sometimes even your conscious beliefs have a way of unconsciously sabotaging you. This happens when they link to unconscious beliefs. Before I was a writer and consultant on conscious awareness and manifestation, I was a personal fitness trainer and rehabilitative specialist for 12 years. During that time period, I developed a strong belief about how good I was at my profession. This belief, in turn, became magnetic to more success and more clientele, further strengthening itself in my consciousness. For many years, I loved what I did and truly enjoyed interacting with many amazing people on a one-on-one basis. I also earned good money and had free time to do extensive research on the power of manifestation. However, there came a point in time when I began to long for something new in my life.

At first, I ignored this underlying feeling of discontentment. After all, I was successful and thriving consistently for the first time in my life. Two years went by while I tried to ignore this feeling. I began to become depressed and fatigued. In my heart I yearned to expand, to do something new and different, but my conscious belief about how successful my business was had linked with unconscious beliefs that I was unaware of. Every time I thought about doing something new, I became fearful and insecure. Sure, most people experience some degree of fear when they consider surrendering the known in lieu of the unknown, but I just couldn't let it go. Instead of loving and enjoying my thriving successful business, or gently and lovingly releasing it without attachment, I was latched onto it out of fear. I began to really notice the problem when my clients started to ask me questions like, "Are you okay?" or "What's on your mind? You don't seem like yourself today, Chris." It was true; I wasn't and hadn't been myself for some time.

What happened was that my unconscious beliefs in lack and limitation had latched onto my conscious belief about how successful I had become as a personal trainer. Beliefs are very tricky in their intricacies and how they can link up with one another. When my worthiness issues latched onto my conscious belief in myself as a successful personal trainer, they demanded that I be grateful for what I got— that I simply take what was given and not question it or expect anything more. The more I contemplated taking a new step into a new and potentially more fulfilling career, the more my worthiness issues continued talking to me at a level I wasn't consciously aware of. They gnawed at me, telling me to hold onto my business, that if I quit training I would be demonstrating my ingratitude towards the Universe.

I had read somewhere that behind every fear there lays a reward. I awoke one morning with this phrase in my mind. I realized how much fear— fear of the unknown, fear of success, and fear of failure— can keep us right where we are. I had put my book project on hold for an entire year, creating excuses about how I should forget trying be to this great writer. That morning, I opened up my laptop and started writing again. The immediate relief I felt when I began to write told me that what I'd needed to do was to *move through my fear*. Further, the reason I was so fearful was that I didn't believe in myself or in my own deservingness and worthiness. This meant *actually claiming a space for myself* in the Universe, not merely taking what I could get. Genuine gratitude for what you have is always, always a good thing. It's a far cry, however, from telling yourself that you need to be grateful for what you are given when it's not what you really want. In this case, you are coming up against your limiting beliefs about how deserving and worthy you are or are not. When I finally began to understand that *behind every fear there lays a reward,* I was finally able to move through my fears and confront my limiting beliefs about my deservingness and worthiness.

Another area where most of us have conflicting conscious and unconscious beliefs is in the area of relationships. Your idea of what a relationship should or shouldn't be is a mix of your conscious and unconscious beliefs. Do you feel like going out and partying on the weekends or would you rather relax with your mate on the couch and watch a movie? Do you want to work with your mate to build something together or are you more independent and would rather work separately to achieve your individual goals? Do you thrive on interaction with other couples or do you thrive on intimacy and alone-time with your mate? Are you traditional in your role of husband and wife, each doing a specific task? Or do you share equally in every area of your lives together? These preferences, which are really beliefs, come from somewhere. In order to create the dream relationship you have always wanted, you will need to become aware of what you are holding onto. It's okay to have preferences, as long as they are coming from a natural judgment or feeling-place of wellness. There is nothing that is not okay, as long as it doesn't harm anyone and is mutually agreed to between partners. It's a matter of choosing to create your relationship from a place of awareness so that you can retain full and healthy control of your Reality Creation.

For me, relationships were the testing grounds to see how much work I still needed to do on myself. Inevitably, you will draw to you the mirror image of yourself, with all the good and all the bad. ***Unearthing the beliefs you have about relationships will facilitate a smoother interaction between yourself and your mate. The more you become aware of potentially limiting beliefs about yourself, and the more you release them, the fewer limiting beliefs your potential partner will have.*** You will always be magnetic to someone who has many of the same emotional issues and core beliefs that you do.

When I was younger, I used to draw partners to myself who had an unconscious belief that love has to be earned. This belief manifests in two ways, both of which represent the same belief. One way this manifests is in the form of a clingy jealous mate who desperately needs your attention all of the time. The other way this manifests is an aloof mate who ignores you much of the time. Both are manifestations of the same belief that *true love must be earned,* and stem from having a distant relationship with your parents. I make mention of this belief again because it operates in our society at a mass level, prolifically wreaking havoc upon millions of relationships. Generally speaking, people with this belief system will enact both roles; either in the scope of a single relationship or throughout the span of many relationships.

What I discovered about myself was that I spent the majority of my time trying to win my partner over and endeavoring to get their full undivided attention. I was in a state of constant yearning for their attention— however, when I finally got that attention, I became disinterested. The reason? It was because I had an unconscious belief that said, "Hey, if you're giving it away, it must not be *real.*" This came from my experiences in childhood; in spite of my constant attempts to get my parent's attention, for the most part, I was ignored. This type of childhood experience forms the building blocks for relationship disaster because no one will ever be able to figure out what you need. Do you want love? Or do you want to chase love? It becomes a vicious cycle of chasing your own tail. Ultimately, the realization of my unconscious beliefs about love began the healing process in my relationships and helped me to transcend that state of unconscious behavior.

My lesson about beliefs was that you have to be willing to look at yourself. Are you doing what you want to be doing or are you holding onto something out of fear? Are you making as much money as you want or are you settling for how much you can get? Do you have a spouse or a mate that loves, supports, and nurtures you or are you living in a fear-based relationship and scared to let go? In order to master your Reality Creation, you will need to unearth the unconscious beliefs you have about yourself and the world at large. As you delve into the work in this book, doing the emotional release exercises and meditation, you will begin to glean a larger picture of yourself. I call this the mile-high view. From this higher perspective and vantage point, many of your previous unconscious belief systems will become consciously visible to you. This book is all about the process of becoming aware of yourself, and through this process you will begin to understand your unconscious and its role in your life. **The unconscious beliefs that you have about life are generally extremely limiting and keep you from creating the life of your dreams. Only when you understand *why* you create what you create can you truly be free to create what you *want* to create.**

≋ 22 ≋

The Mass Mind

AGAIN, EVERY PERSON emits their own personal energy field. This energy field emanates from them, extending outwards around them. Your personal vibrational energetic field, as we have learned, is comprised of your conscious *and* unconscious intentions, a mixture of all your emotions, thoughts, and feelings, ultimately harmonizing into one vibrational field that is you. The same can be said for a group of people, as well. When a group of people get together, they have a tendency to synchronize or equalize their vibrational rate. Thus, their individual energy bodies begin to merge as one larger energy body. Over time, this energy begins to assume an identity of sorts and comes alive. It can be likened to a rather large sub-personality, except that it is more of a mass personality. This is also different from the *collective consciousness* of mankind. Within the collective consciousness exists all of the streams of consciousness of mankind, a Universal Record of all the thoughts ever to be thought of.

The Mass Mind exists rather, as the *collective unconscious* of a populace in any given area. It feeds and thrives off of lower vibrational thoughts and emotions. Just as your pain body, or sub personality will become active to feed itself, so will the Mass Mind. This energy body can exist as a nation, or even as small as a single family. There is an energy body around every single person and around every single group of people. As much as a person may find it difficult to pull away from the energy of their family in their attempts to succeed at life, a person could find it difficult to overcome the unconsciousness of an area. For example, if you lived within a crime-ridden, poverty-stricken neighborhood, you might find it difficult to become successful. Indeed, you may find it near impossible because every time you make a step in the right direction, you find yourself fighting against the very people around you. The Mass Mind consciousness of the area is saturated with beliefs in limitation and negativity. For some people, this is quite alright. Remember, there are no judgments, only that which serves your highest purpose and that which does not. However, if you desire to achieve growth and expansion in your life, you may need to leave the area.

The same thing can be said of an individual family. I personally know of countless examples of people having to completely separate themselves from the family that they grew up in, in order to achieve their goals. If a family is stricken with limiting negative beliefs about themselves and/or the world at large, they will hold this as an unconscious energy body. This energy becomes the Mass Mind of this family and takes on a life of its own. Thus, when someone tries to break free, this energy body becomes active as it now feels threatened. It will utilize whichever person is most susceptible to negativity and unconsciousness within the family to attack the threat. It will do whatever it can to defend itself and stay alive. If, for example, one family member breaks free, relocates themselves, and becomes successful, it could lead to others doing the same thing. If this begins to happen, this energy body will start to diminish and lose its sustenance. And, anytime you elevate yourself in any way, you lessen the likelihood of generating negative thoughts and emotions. Thus, for some individuals, the first biggest struggle could be perceived as against their own family. In actuality, however, it's not against their family, but rather against the collective unconsciousness of their family. Using the term 'pain body' as defined by Eckhart Tolle in his book *The Power of Now*, the collective unconsciousness is simply a larger version of the pain body. It is, in essence, the 'family pain body'. Any time somebody elevates or attempts to elevate themselves above the masses, whether it's within their own family or within their country, they must transcend the Mass Mind consciousness. You might say it's a test of will power. However, if you recognize what is happening, it need not take will power.

As an example, even within my own family, I encountered our Mass Mind consciousness. We were poor and we loved it! In actuality, *we* didn't really love it, our *family pain body* loved it. There was always justification and rationalization for our poverty consciousness. This, in turn, would perpetually feed our family pain body. When I was younger, and much before I began the path of self-awareness, I enacted this Mass Mind consciousness myself. After many years of struggle and strife, my mother finally began to enjoy a modicum of success. At the time I was no longer living at home, but interestingly enough I felt very much that I should be enjoying part of that success as well. After all, I had suffered as a child not having all of the things that my friends did. Thus, I began to call and beg for money at least once a month. Outwardly, it may have appeared innocent enough: a son asking his mother for money. But on a deeper level, it is not unusual to see this dynamic manifesting in families that have a massive amount of poverty consciousness: when one family member has just started to taste success, other family members will suddenly and mysteriously appear to need money. What is happening here is that the unconscious sabotage mechanism, or collective unconsciousness of the family, is becoming active. In this scenario, as one family member begins to rise up, all of the others suddenly grab a hold and begin to pull back down. This mechanism is totally and completely unconscious, no one aware of what they are really doing.

Of course, years later when I began to taste success, I also felt the pull of the family Mass Mind consciousness or collective unconsciousness on myself, as well.

Mysteriously, when I bought my first brand new car, which was a metallic quartz blue 330ci BMW, I received more than a few telephone calls asking for money. When this happens, you may have to exhibit some tough love with your family. In this case, if you attempt to help someone before you are firmly entrenched within your newly-found success, you are just going to energetically drain yourself. On top of this, you will only feed the Mass Mind consciousness of your family. You are in actuality not feeding the family; you are feeding their collective emotional wounds and belief systems. There is no satiating an empty emotional hole. You can pour all the resources into it you want, it will yet remain. During the time I was attempting to beggar resources off my mom, she eventually did the single best thing she could have done for herself and for me. It remains to this day one of the single greatest lessons I have ever learned.

One evening I called my mom to begin my begging again. She paused and asked me the following question, "Chris, how much is enough for you?" As she did not ask it in a friendly way, I said nothing back. Instead, I became sulky and withdrawn. Further, I attempted to guilt- trip her into sending me more money. She did not fall for it, though, and stood firm in her resolve. For a couple of months after that, I pouted and stayed angry at her. However, after about three months, I shook it off and an amazing thing happened. I got a better job and became more self-sustaining. My mom had liberated me, with tough love, from the Mass Mind poverty consciousness that had kept our family stuck in a rut for generations. Although I began to realize the power of what she had done for me, it wasn't until later on that I understood the dynamics of what had happened and how we are intimately connected to the different energy bodies around us.

Another dynamic in the Mass Mind is that it is always stronger wherever there is more pain and suffering. This only makes good sense when you remember that its other name is the 'pain body', or the 'Mass Mind pain body.' Again, it needs emotional suffering in order to feed itself. When people are confronted with a physical reality that is much less than desirable, the suffering that results can create *beliefs* in suffering and limitation. This is the recipe to a triple- layer soufflé for the Mass Mind and it will greedily devour all of the suffering these beliefs generate. Every group of people, every neighborhood, every city, every town, every club, every weekly meeting, every cult, every family, every nation, emanates a collective unconscious energy body that we call the Mass Mind. Some of these Mass Mind pain bodies are very light with much less negativity, while others are darker and heavier with more negativity.

Another way you may encounter the Mass Mind is through mass belief systems. If you are on the bus, you sneeze and the person next to you says, "It's goin' around," you have encountered the Mass Mind. If your knee hurts and someone says you should get arthroscopic surgery, you have encountered the Mass Mind. If you are having trouble with your finances and someone tells you to join the crowd, you have encountered the Mass Mind. If you decide to tell one of your friends that you want to become a millionaire and they tell you to get real, you have encountered the Mass Mind. When someone tells you that it's time we got rid of them Iraqis once and for all, you have encountered the Mass Mind. Any time you encounter people enacting and reacting to mass belief systems, you are in the midst of the Mass Mind. In essence, it is akin to being plugged into an automated system that keeps you right exactly where you are in life. If you want to transcend the Mass Mind, you will need to unplug from the Mass Mind belief systems that feed it.

The best way I have personally found to elevate yourself beyond the Mass Mind is to simply not buy into it. Your first step is always, of course, the awareness that you have been plugged in up until now. You will need to be aware of how you, yourself, have been a part of the Mass Mind and have been living through it. It will also help you to remember that it's not black and white, as you elevate your conscious awareness, you transcend a little more each time. You decide not to buy into it by not believing in all of the limitation that everyone else around you may be preaching. You may decide not to listen to the nightly news that feeds the Mass Mind with massive amounts of limiting belief systems. If you have an idea, a dream to build a business or do something big with your life, you may decide instead to keep it to yourself. After all, do you need someone else to believe in your idea or are you ready to *be* your idea? It always helps to have other people support you in your efforts, but you will always risk encountering the Mass Mind if you go on and on about your great idea to anyone who will listen. Inevitably, you will encounter people who are plugged in that will tell you to forget it, face the facts, and get real. Reality *is* whatever *you* make it to be, but not everyone is ready to accept that. Accepting that you create your reality is also accepting responsibility for yourself. Thus, you will need to accept responsibility for creating your own success and becoming self-sustaining if you wish to transcend Mass Mind consciousness.

Have you ever felt like there was some force working against your best efforts to change? Let's say you decide you want to rise above your current situation, circumstance, or even peer group. Again, there is no judgment about where you or anyone else is, let's just assume that you have come to the realization that you want to expand yourself. As you begin to undergo this process, you may encounter resistance from other people around you. A great example is when one member of a group of social drinkers decides that they want to cut back on their alcohol drinking. This is an easy example to illustrate because most people know or have known someone in this situation. Not only does this person have to face their own unconscious compulsions and inner saboteur, but they now have to face all of their friends' unconscious mechanisms, as well. Dealing with this level of inner and outer resistance can make someone feel as though they are trying to climb Mt. Everest, on their own, without any gear and with no arms or legs.

There are a growing number of beliefs instilled within the Mass Mind that stifle growth and creativity. These beliefs are called *mass beliefs*. Here are some examples of widely-accepted mass beliefs:

- The belief in limitation: there are not enough resources to go around
- Only a few people can be rich and wealthy
- There is such a thing as cold and flu season
- The inevitability of disease
- Life is a struggle
- God's love has to be earned
- One group of people is more deserving than another
- Competition is necessary
- You have to prove yourself, you must earn the right to be here
- Might makes right

Any belief that is held by the masses as true, regardless of whether or not someone else has proven it to be untrue or not, is a mass belief. You could even just narrow it down to phrases like:

"Money doesn't grow on trees."

"Face the facts."

"It's Monday."

"Must be nice."

"Get used to it."

You could also call these phrases "victim statements" with equal accuracy since they ignore the truth, which is that we control our reality, not the other way around.

I encountered a woman in the gym once who was a brilliant example of mass beliefs in action. (This actually happens quite frequently to everyone, all you have to do is pay attention to what people are really saying to you.) I happened to be sniffling, just ever so slightly. She walked up to me and said, "Are you sick?" What a *strange* thing to say, I thought, since that day I felt great, had a ton of energy, and was ready to conquer the world. So I said, "No, are *you*?" She suddenly looked very offended, turned, and stalked off.

When people are plugged into the Mass Mind, they want you to play along. The Mass Mind thrives on lack and limitation. A sure way to offend someone is to disagree with them when they are plugged in. And yet, in order to become a conscious creator, you will need to transcend all of the beliefs in limitation around you. This may mean that you can no longer play along anymore. When someone tells you that life is a struggle and yet you know that we have the choice to create our lives the way we want to, you have come to a critical point. Outwardly and blatantly disagreeing with someone seldom brings about the highest good for all involved. It will, in fact, only serve to diminish your vibrational energetic field. Since you do not wish to verbally agree with this person— because you know your words are powerful— and you also do not wish to disagree with them— because you do not want to create conflict— your best option may be to give a gentle suggestion.

What I like to do in this circumstance, especially when someone is visibly waiting for you to agree with them, is to give an option like, "Maybe." I like this approach because it does not create resistance in the other party, which only serves to lower your vibrational energetic field. Responding this way also reinforces within your own mind the fact that you know you create your reality. Or, if during the delicate process of separating yourself from the Mass Mind, someone really wants to argue with you about some Mass Mind belief they are espousing, you can always give them the most inarguable point you could ever make. Simply tell them that is not what *you believe*. You wouldn't even want to tell them that your beliefs are different, because this will still create conflict with someone who is dead set on being right. The one thing they cannot argue with is what you believe. You cannot change someone's beliefs by force, ever. Since inherently everyone recognizes this, it is always your failsafe to protect yourself from environmental conflict with people who are still plugged in.

You have to be a bit selective about what you share with people who are really plugged into the Mass Mind belief system. The stronger the belief in limitation, the stronger the reaction you will get if you challenge their belief. You don't want to respond to the insane homeless guy on the street who asks you for money by telling him that he creates his own reality, he may flip out on you. When you start gaining awareness about beliefs, you may wish to remember two golden rules that I attempt to live by:

Rule number one: "The best advice given is advice asked for.

Rule number two: "If you want to lead, lead by example."

Your only job is to work on *you* and unplug yourself from the belief in limitation. You will not have to chase people down and tell them that they need to unplug from limitation. The people who want to change will be inspired and drawn to you by your ability to go against the perceived odds to create your life the way you want to. When someone comes to you and asks you how you have achieved such an amazing life, then you can tell them. They will be more ready to receive the gift of freedom now that you are in a position to give.

≋ 23 ≋

Localized Mass Mind

T HERE ARE ALSO mass beliefs that are localized to various regions around the world. People in different countries face different challenges according to the belief systems that are held by the majority of people in that area. For example, in some countries in Africa, you are literally lucky to survive with both arms and legs. It is widely agreed amongst many of the people in these countries that *this is just the way life is.* In order to effect change, a person would be going up against that particular mass belief. Great leaders have emerged to lead peoples and nations to victory. However, it is also clear that these particular souls incarnated for that particular purpose. Most people are still working on creating their own life the way *they* want it, minus the fact that they may be in an area where the accepted way of life is far from the way that *anyone* would want it.

Sometimes, it will be necessary to extract yourself from certain areas, both locally and regionally, if you wish to elevate yourself above the mass consciousness. If there is mortar fire going off around you or the neighbor's kids just died of starvation, your first priority might be to leave the country. Sure, it's easy to rattle off this advice while safely within the confines of a wealthy nation. And yet, many people have already done this exact thing, and indeed made it happen by focusing their attention upon what they wanted. Perhaps, after you have elevated your consciousness to the necessary level, you may return and emerge as a great leader, bringing needed change to an entire country or nation. You will not be able to do this until you, yourself, have transcended the Mass Mind and mastered the ability to create your own reality first. Thus, in some cases, it would be necessary to leave an area, spend some time building up your vibrational energetic field in a more hospitable environment, then return when you are able to effect change. Is the energy you are in or around compatible to living the life of your dreams? Otherwise, you may energetically deplete yourself trying to create something that is not supported by your environment and the mass beliefs of the area.

An example of this type of situation would be living in a neighborhood that does not match your vibrational rate of attraction. It could be the energy of the people or the energy of the land, itself. Everyone has a personal preference as to their ideal living situation and when you are out of accord with that you will drain your vibrational energetic field. Conversely, when you take the time to find the neighborhood and area that you are a vibrational match to, you serve to enhance and increase your vibrational energetic field. Any time you feel resistance to the area around you, you are not in alignment with the flow of energy. It is important to be in harmony with the energy of the people or the area where you are living because it will help you to stay in the flow and purposefully create your reality with greater ease.

Section Three: Clearing And Healing

"There comes that time when the soul must once again leave the sanctuary of the spirit world for another trip to Earth. This decision is not an easy one. Souls must prepare to leave a world of total wisdom, where they exist in a blissful state of freedom, for the physical and mental demands of a human body." —Journey of Souls

Dr. Michael Newton, PH.D.

≋ 24 ≋

The Importance of Clearing

I N ORDER TO master your Reality Creation, you will
need to clear and heal your emotional, mental, and
physical bodies. These three areas comprise the
actual density within your bio-energetic sphere. Your
thoughts and emotions are actual things. They have a
molecular weight to them, much as protons and elec-
trons. Your mental and emotional bodies exist, yet you
cannot see either one of them. Your physical body you
can see, of course, because it is physical. However, a
thing need not be manifest in the physical in order for
it to have a density to it. Energy, in and of itself, is a non
physical phenomenon and yet has a certain density to it.
Even though you can only see one of these three bodies,
they all three need clearing and healing.

The road to mastery begins with awareness of self.
Have you ever looked in the mirror and asked the question, "Who am I?" It's kind of unsettling when you

realize that you may not really know the answer. Most people are living in a costume that they never take off. The problem is that the costume is restrictive and only allows you to play a certain role by certain rules. You can never truly live out your dreams while wearing this costume. Clearing yourself will help you to dismantle the costume and experience the unlimited version of you that's underneath. It does not happen overnight. Rather, it is through the process of being consistent in your dedication to releasing your emotional wounds, inputting positive commands into your subconscious, and clearing yourself, that you will begin to witness an augmented reality.

≋ 25 ≋

Clearing the Emotional Body

I USE THREE primary methods for clearing and healing. They are: *Meditation, Affirmation,* and *Release
Work.* You will benefit greatly from doing any one
of these practices. The integration of all three will make
you unstoppable in the pursuit of your dream life. People are born with a bright, shiny little magnet in the core
of their being. Clearing your emotional body is like pol-
ishing the dirt off of the magnet so that you only draw to
yourself what you want.

Your emotional body consists of emotional wounds,
beliefs, and the feelings associated with the wounds
and beliefs. Clearing the emotional body can be extremely rewarding for those people who are holding
onto all of their old emotional baggage. This unhealed
energy can literally create a blockade that will not allow
energy to flow into your life. It can also sit within you at a
deeply unconscious level and magnetize like-vibrational

people, places, and events to you. This is really bothersome because you can continuously draw a negative circumstance to yourself and not know that it comes from deep inside of you. Thus, healing and releasing your emotional body can give you great creative freedom.

≋ 26 ≋

Meditation

B EFORE YOU BEGIN to gain emotional freedom, you will need to disengage your mind. So many people torture themselves continuously with an ongoing barrage of never-ending thoughts. I cannot personally think of any worse affliction than not being able to stop thinking. Without proper rest from the mind, you will eventually develop some sort of neurosis or depression. Traditionally, you are supposed to be able to get this break from your mind when you sleep at night. However, most people in this day and age do not get near their proper sleep requirements, if they get any sleep at all. Stress, stimulants, deadlines, and the desire to achieve more, drive people upwards and onwards at all costs. People are even willing to forgo their health in favor of achieving more financial rewards.

To combat this and gain a foothold over your emotional highs and lows, I recommend you begin with

20 minutes of meditation in the morning. Remember, you are here to become the master of your Reality Creation, so get ready to do the work. I recommend using the "So-Hum" Mantra Meditation. After teaching this meditation to a number of people and witnessing first-hand the amazing results, I became convinced of the powerful effects it can have. It is also an easy meditation to master and a great first step for people who are new to meditation. When I first began meditation, it was purely for the enhancement of my success. What I found was, not only did I make more money and become more successful, but I also became more peaceful and expended a lot less energy trying to get things done.

So Hum Mantra Meditation

- ✤ Sit in a quiet place, comfortably relaxed and upright, making sure you will not be disturbed (turn off phones). You do not need to hold a rigid posture for this type of meditation (in fact when I do this meditation, I lean against the wall to support my lower back).
- ✤ Close your eyes and take a couple of deep breaths, get even more relaxed.
- ✤ After a minute, you will begin to mentally whisper the word "so" when you inhale and the word "hum" when you exhale, making sure you breathe in and out through your nose.
- ✤ Do not force the breath; do not try to resonate the breath with the words. Instead it's the other way around. Breathe naturally through the nose,

then let the words resonate with the breath, gently whispering "so" mentally in your mind when you inhale and "hum" mentally in your mind when you exhale.

- If you find yourself thinking about something, do not be discouraged. Instead, gently bring yourself back to the mantra.
- Eventually, the mantra may disappear and you may experience a deeper peace, floating, expansion, and other varied states of consciousness, all of which are a sign of productive meditation. If the mantra disappears at some point and you feel your presence growing, allow the process.
- Results will appear gradually in your life, thus the best meditation practice is a consistent meditation practice.
- Stick with 20 minutes a day in the morning for the first three months. Afterwards, add another 20 minutes in the late afternoon or early evening.
- "So Hum" or "Ham So" means "I am that" or "I am the Divine," so you are eliciting the divinity within yourself when you say this mantra.

When I first began meditating, I noticed subtle yet profound results in my life. One of the things that happens when you meditate is that everything in your life suddenly becomes easier and your efforts become more successful. After my first three weeks of consistent meditation, my life changed so dramatically that I got caught up in my newfound success and quit meditating. What I didn't realize was that it was *because* of the meditation that I was more successful. So, after a couple of weeks with no meditation practice, I began to notice that life seemed harder again. It took me awhile to put it all together. It's so subtle that you can easily fool yourself into believing something other than the truth. The truth for me was that I doubled my success by meditating, but then back-pedaled in my progress when I stopped meditating.

Another amazing thing that happens from meditation is that you become less reactive. In other words, you begin to diffuse your *reactive unconscious behavior*. **When you allow your mind to rest with meditation, your psyche has a chance to heal itself and you gain emotional clarity. Suddenly, things that were a really big deal and really bothering you don't matter nearly as much. When you quit unconsciously reacting to everything around you, there is suddenly space to make conscious choices. This new-found awareness will bring you a more solid foundation for taking command of your Reality Creation.**

≋ 27 ≋

The Spoken Word

EVERY TIME YOU speak a word, you are verbalizing and solidifying a thought. Solidifying a thought with your words causes it to manifest into form. The truth is, when a thought arises within your mind, it is offering itself to you as an option to manifest into form. You sift through thousands of thoughts a day, picking and choosing which ones you want to give attention to. When you use affirmations and speak the Word aloud, you are purposefully bringing desired thoughts into form. This is also a good way to cut through mental clutter. As you continue to speak only of that which you wish to experience, you will become very powerful. Any thought spoken aloud consistently enough will come to manifest as a physical thing or event. Your ability to consistently speak of your desired outcome will help you master the ability to direct nonphysical energy into physical form.

Affirmations are one of the single most powerful and often overlooked ways of effecting change in your life. You could transcend all limitation with the power of the spoken word alone. Personally, I used to scoff at the idea of affirmations because it was such an intangible, esoteric idea with no large body of evidence to support it. However, after I read *The Power of Your Subconscious Mind* by Dr. Joseph Murphy, I decided to try affirmations in earnest. When I really applied affirmations, consistently on a daily basis, I began to make dramatic changes in my life. I noticed that I felt better, was more decisive, and was able to create more opportunity for myself.

Affirmations are a great way to cut through the Mass Mind, as well. The Mass Mind is most effective when you are unclear of what you want or when you feel confused and emotionally unstable. In this state of confusion and emotional instability, you are most vulnerable to negative limited thinking. However, when you use affirmations, you become impenetrable to mass beliefs and negative emotional states. People cannot affect you with their limiting ideas about the state of the world or what you should do with your life. The more you practice affirmations, the more precise and effective you will be in creating your life exactly the way you want it.

One of the first things I noticed when I began doing affirmations consistently was that I felt like I was literally creating my reality with my words. I noticed, however, that after several days of not doing the affirmations, my Reality Creation would begin to crumble and fall apart.

At first I was really despondent and began to despair, thinking that affirmations were a big load of cow dung. When I started doing the affirmations again, I again noticed the positive results after about three days. My first thought was, *"Gee wiz, am I going to have to do affirmations every day for the rest of my life?!"* My second thought was, *"Am I really complaining about having to say a few words every day to create my dream life?"* And there it was; I suddenly realized that, like anything else in life, consistency equals results. In order to create changes that last a lifetime, you will need to dedicate your life and your actions to creating the changes you want.

Emotional Affirmation Exercise
- I am happy, joyous, and free.
- I am radiant and abundant, attracting more wealth to me every day.
- I am strong, powerful, and healthy.

Again, be consistent. Do it every single day. If you do, you will get results. If you don't, you will not get results. These particular affirmations are more generalized, which makes them more effective for elevating and stabilizing your emotional state. When I do my affirmations, I like to integrate into them into my daily routine, usually just after meditation. I generally try to do affirmations three times a day, every day. However, because emotional affirmations can help you in the moment, it can also be helpful to do them any time you are not feeling emotionally stable. Thus, emotional affirmations can be used either in a routine or through-out the day depending upon your needs.

Key Points
- ✓ When you say an affirmation, say it out loud to yourself.
- ✓ Try to state your affirmation with as much feeling as you can muster. If you are really down or depressed, then just do the best you can and it will still have a positive impact.
- ✓ Remember to be consistent, meaning that you will need to say your affirmations on a daily basis. Generally, three times a day is the minimum to effect change.
- ✓ Remember, the affirmation you are saying may not be true for you in this moment. That's the whole point, you are working at effecting change, so release your judgment about whether it's true or not.
- ✓ When it comes to emotional affirmations, use a barrage of them to create the biggest change.
- ✓ Say the previously mentioned affirmations a minimum of three times a day out loud to yourself. Remember that it usually takes three days before changes occur in your life.

≋ 28 ≋

Emotional Release

THE NEXT STEP in the process of emotional clearing and taking charge of your Reality Creation is to facilitate the release of all of your old emotional baggage. Ultimately, if you were to clear *all* your emotional baggage, with this one step you could completely master your ability to manifest, as you would become crystal clear. There would be no confusion about what you want and you would have no emotional pitfalls to sabotage yourself with. However, if it were that easy, a lot more people would have already done this. Like everything else in life you want to achieve, you will need to work consistently to clear yourself using emotional release techniques.

A big part of the process of understanding emotional release is understanding the relationship between your negative emotions—anger, jealousy, fear, envy, lust, etc.—to any pain in your body. If you have any physical ailments or aches and pains in your body, you probably have stored emotional baggage. Wherever there is pain or tension in your body, you can bet it relates to the unhealed emotional energy that is being stored in that particular part of the body. In other words, your unhealed emotional wounds can literally sit inside different areas of your body and manifest as physical ailments. Here is a hint: I haven't met anyone, ever, anywhere, who wasn't holding onto some sort of emotional baggage, me included.

Stored emotional baggage affects your vibrational field and vibrational rate of attraction. As your vibrational energy field is constantly radiating out from you, you definitely want to make sure that you are sending the clearest signal you can. Your stored emotional energy is emitting a signal that is most likely drawing situations to you that you do not want. Generally speaking, nobody wants unpaid bills, an abusive partner, or confrontations with angry people at the grocery store. However, your unhealed, unconscious stored emotional energy will draw exactly these kinds of circumstances to you.

Do you ever wonder why some days you have to really try to stay positive? It's because this energy becomes active when you haven't acted out on it in a long time. In the section on the Mass Mind, we talked about the *pain body*. As we discussed, this negative emotional energy, or pain body, needs you to feed it in order to stay alive. So, sometimes it will literally become active and magnetize people, places, or circumstances to you that are designed to get you to react unconsciously, in a negative way, to feed it its sustenance. Its sustenance is your own negative lower vibrational emotional energy. In other words, your pain body needs to get you to feel negative in order to stay alive. Part of the process of releasing your emotional baggage is actively starving out the pain body.

My three favorite teachers of emotional release are Eckhart Tolle, Hale Dwoskin, and Brad Yates. In his book, *Practicing the Power of Now*, Eckhart Tolle teaches how to become aware of the pain body and how it feeds off of your negativity. In his book, *The Sedona Method*, Hale Dwoskin describes his technique for *allowing* yourself to release negative emotions. Brad Yates has taken EFT, or Emotional Freedom Technique, to a whole new level by allowing you to do online EFT through his website. Ultimately, you will need to discover which techniques work best for you to heal and clear your emotional body. What I offer is a basic release technique that I created myself as an integration of several techniques.

Emotional Release Technique #1

- ∾ First, find a relaxing place to sit where you will not be disturbed.
- ∾ Take two deep breathes and relax.
- ∾ Close your eyes and just sit for a moment.
- ∾ Now, pick an area of your life that is troubling you right now. It can be anything, ranging from your relationship, your finances, your physical body, or painful memories. You want to generally start, however, with what is bothering you the most in this moment.

- Allow yourself to fully feel all of the emotion be-hind this issue.

- See if you can completely allow this scenario to unfold in your mind, no matter how painful it is. In other words, do not offer any resistance to it.

- Now, see if you can completely allow it to be there, 100%, and allow yourself to experience the emotions without identifying with them.

- Know that your emotions are not you, they are what you experience. When you completely detach from identification with your emotions, then you can release them.

- Now, ask yourself if you are willing to release these emotions.

- Give yourself a minute or more after asking your-self this question; let it settle in. Do not try to answer this question for yourself, instead allow yourself to be guided.

- It doesn't matter whether the answer is yes or no, just stay relaxed and allow.

- One of the ways you'll know if this technique is working is if you feel lighter afterward, more peaceful. If you still feel some or all of the emo-tion, that is ok. You may wish to repeat the re-lease a few times.

- After you're done, do some emotional affirma-tions to assure that you are still in command of your Reality Creation.

Emotional Release Technique #2 (On-The-Spot Release)

- Use this technique when something triggers your emotional pain body while you are going about your day. In other words, if someone or something suddenly triggers you emotionally, you can release it right then and there.

- If this has just happened, the first thing you need to do is find a place where you are comfortable. If you cannot leave the area, then do the best you can.

- Within your mind, see if you can allow yourself to experience the emotion that was triggered and remain relaxed at the same time.

- Now, go within that emotion and see if you can allow yourself to go deep down inside of it, as much as you can.

- Ask yourself mentally or out loud, "Could I allow myself to go deeply within this emotion?" When you do this, allow yourself some time and try to stay as relaxed as possible.

- When you go deeply enough within the emotion, you will release it.

- Sometimes you will release a little bit, sometimes a lot, and sometimes you can release an entire emotional issue inside of two minutes!

- After you are done, check yourself to see how you're feeling. If you are feeling good, chances are you got a good release. If you feel emotional, then chances are you need to do some more release work.

When I first began doing emotional release work, I could not believe how simplistically profound it was. I clearly remember the time I used it after having an egoic staredown with another guy in the gym. My insecurity had gotten the better of me and I succumbed to the staring game with a guy who was working out in the same area of the gym as I was. He stared at me again and I tried to ignore it. I was fuming at this outrage, *how dare he assume this aggressive posture with me*!? Suddenly, I remembered this technique and decided I would try it. I left the gym, went out to my car, sat down and closed my eyes. I felt the anger and rage I had towards this guy. I allowed myself to just feel these emotions as strongly as I could. Next, I asked myself if I could release it. To my amazing surprise, I began to feel the energy actually travel through my body, upwards and out. In that moment, I felt lighter and more peaceful. I was amazed that it could be this easy!

The next thing that happened was that I realized under my anger was great fear. In that instant, I suddenly understood that a lot of my anger was as a result of feeling fearful all of the time. So then I applied the same technique to the fear. Again, I felt some energy leaving my body. Not as much as the first time, but still significant. Today, I utilize this technique constantly and notice that I have fewer and fewer emotional issues in my life, overall. I even used it one time when I felt my heart was beating too hard in my chest. After I applied the emotional release technique, my heart actually began to beat more softly. Incredible.

≋ 29 ≋

Clearing the Mental Body

I N HIS GROUNDBREAKING book, *Evolve your Brain*, Joe Dispenza, D.C. refers to your *neural networks*, which I will shorten to *neural net*. Your mental body is composed of your neural net, or your habitual thought patterns. As it turns out, thinking in certain patterns can become addictive. When we think different thoughts, our brain fires different neural patterns, which trigger different biochemical states in our body. Releasing these different chemicals over and over again creates a dependency that results in addiction to the certain types of thoughts that lead to certain types of behaviors. This is also one of the reasons why it can take effort to actually control your thoughts; it's like fighting a chemical dependency.

≋ 30 ≋

Controlling Your Thoughts

P URPOSEFULLY CONTROLLING YOUR thoughts can be extremely difficult. Instead of forcing anything at all, begin to discern the nature of your thoughts. The first step towards controlling your thoughts is to understand the difference between a positive and a negative thought. Another way of looking at it is to understand the difference between a productive thought and an unproductive thought. *Every thought you think has an outcome attached to it. Every outcome you can think of will either move you up the ladder in a productive way or move you down the ladder in a negative direction.* Basically, anything you think that does not promote yours or someone else's health and well being is an unproductive or negative thought.

Next, you need to understand how to identify the difference between a positive and negative thought when they arise within your mind. Luckily for us, we all have a built-in inner sense of well being that tells us when we are feeling or being negative. It's our *feeling power*. Every time you generate a thought, you intuitively know—immediately, through your feelings—whether it's positive or negative. If you are dwelling upon a particular subject matter and you are not feeling good about it, chances are you have involved yourself in a negative thought process. On top of that, you are most likely focused upon an outcome that you do not want as opposed to one that you do.

As an example, I used to think about how I could get back at people whom I felt had wronged me in some way. The problem was that it never felt good to think about the ways in which I would get them back. Also, I noticed that the more negatively I thought about them, the more likely I was to magnetize this person right back into my life. Not only that, but thinking about them in a negative way would ensure that I would magnetize them in a negative way. *My bad-feeling thoughts led to bad-feeling outcomes.* At first, I was resistant to the idea of thinking positively about people I thought were negative. After I tried it, though, I realized that was the only way to live. I began to think more positive thoughts about everyone, including the people who I had previously referred to as negative. Low and behold, people began to act more positively towards *me*! It's amazing to see how addicted to negative thinking you can become and the amazing transformation that results when you begin to think positively.

I remember this guy who used to be a personal trainer at the gym where I trained my clients. In essence, you could call us coworkers, even though we were independent contractors and not employed by the gym. Thus, we would encounter each other every day. Also, we both worked six days a week, which meant that we ended up spending a lot of time together in a small, studio-sized gym. We hated each other. It was mostly just the usual stuff, egoic, macho crap type stuff. However, I decided that I wanted to see if I could change our interactions without ever saying anything to him. I was playing around with the positive thinking a bit and starting visualizing the two of us laughing and smiling together. It wasn't easy because, well, I hated him. At the time, I would much rather have gotten into a physical fight with this guy instead of trying to think of anything positive about him. However, I spent this particular morning visualizing the two of us laughing and carrying on together as if we were lifelong buds. I got to the gym and just couldn't believe it when he smiled at me and said, "Hey Chris." Not only that, but there was no malice or cutting joke, either within the greeting or afterwards. He seemed....*happy*! Now, I've had my ups and downs with this technique, mostly because it requires great discipline to do it every single day. However, I had learned my lesson. I was the one in charge of my Reality Creation, nobody else. I could choose my destiny every single day if I wanted to.

Afterwards, the most astounding discovery was actually in the realization of how many times throughout the day I was having negative thoughts about people, places, and circumstances. On top of that, my validation and rationalization for my negativity was masterful in and of itself. I would come up with the most elaborate reasons for having negative, limiting thoughts about people and situations. The moment I began truly working towards having more positive thoughts rather than negative ones was the moment I started to turn my life around.

Thought Redirection Exercise

- Think about someone with whom you have had a disagreement or some friction.
- Challenge yourself and see if you can find something good about this person. In other words, pick something that is good about them to focus upon.
- Now, think about how you would like that person to be in your life.
- Feel the joy of smiling and laughing with this person.
- Next, pay attention to the results of your efforts. Your new thoughts will create a new reality.
- You will be projecting a higher version of this person into your reality and reap a more rewarding, productive outcome.

≋ 31 ≋

Re-Patterning Your Neural Net

<hr>

A FTER YOU HAVE spent some time working on redirecting your thoughts towards productive and
positive outcomes, you can then begin to work
on re-patterning your neural net. You do this by gaining
more knowledge, learning new skills and establishing
new ways of living. In other words, you need to enact
new behaviors and ways of thinking in order to develop
a new neural net. In addition, if you want to create a new
expanded neural net, you need to *consistently* enact new
behaviors and ways of thinking. Changing your behavior
and becoming a positive thinker for a day just won't cut it.
You will need to develop the consistent habit of thinking
in new ways and opening up to new ideas. Once you see
the results this new habit produces, you will be inspired
to permanently adopt it into your lifestyle.

What I noticed about myself is that after I had been
redirecting my thoughts for one week, not only did I

manifest new and incredible things in my life, but I also found that it was easier to maintain those positive-feeling thoughts the following week. So my progress was cumulative. In this way you also can build upon your progress; each positive thought upon the next. And, it DOES get easier.

At one point in my life, I had become the most negative person I knew. I was severely depressed and extremely cynical. When I first started redirecting my thoughts and reconstructing my neural net, it was like trying to walk through quicksand with cement boots on. I felt like I weighed 1,000 pounds, every step of the way. But even though I was exhausted, I kept at it. Amazingly, after only three days of redirecting my thoughts towards the positive, I began to see results. I felt better, not quite as depressed and cynical. Also, I started magnetizing more financial opportunities into my life again.

For two years I had been experiencing the worst depression in my life and now in the span of three days I had begun to reverse the cycle. The work was not done, however. I lapsed on my positive thinking and affirmations and it only took a couple days before I began to spiral back downwards into depression and gloom. It was so overwhelming that I nearly forgot how I had started to break out of my vicious cycle. When I realized that I wasn't redirecting my thoughts and doing my affirmations, I quickly began anew. This time I stuck with it until I felt great and also had a full thriving business to match my good feelings. It *did* work for me; I just needed to maintain consistency to maintain my results.

Re-Patterning Exercise

- Pick one thing that you want to change about yourself. It could be to smile at people instead of frown, taking the time to give each one of your kids a hug in the morning, saying something nice to a coworker, staying calm in traffic instead of being angry, or even something bigger, like learning a new language.

- Now, be consistent with this exercise, meaning, practice this new behavior *every day*.

- After one week, notice how much better you feel and how you are attracting more positive circumstances to yourself.

- Your new way of thinking will create a new neural net, making positive changes easier to make.

- Ultimately, you will want to challenge yourself more and more, changing new behaviors and creating a completely new neural net and a completely new you.

≋ 32 ≋

Affirming the Life You Want

Y OU CAN USE affirmations on the mental body, as
well. When you use affirmations on the mental
body, you are enhancing your neural net, plant-
ing the seeds for higher vibrational emotions and taking
conscious control of your Reality Creation. Any time
you consciously input a positive command into your
mental body, you are elevating your vibrational rate of
attraction. The more you do this, the more beneficial
and positive your results will be.

Inserting positive commands into your mental body
through the use of affirmations will ultimately result in
total control of your reality creation. *When you take
charge of your life by consciously choosing the thoughts
and thought patterns you want in your mind, you will
experience the outer reflection of this choice in the physical world around you. Even if you had to do this every
day on a daily basis for the rest of your life, wouldn't it*

be worth it to be in total control of every aspect of your life? To me, the answer was a big "YES!" Affirmations helped to turn my life around and led me to total control of my reality creation. Using affirmations to maximize the power of my mind greatly accelerated the "rate of return" as I worked to create the reality I truly wanted.

Key Points
- ✓ Say affirmations out loud to yourself for mental power and clarity.
- ✓ Say them every day for a minimum of three times a day throughout the day.
- ✓ Remember, at least three days may be necessary in order for you to begin to notice the positive effects in your reality creation.

Mental Affirmation Exercise
- ❧ I am clear, precise, and exact in every moment.
- ❧ I am ultimate power.
- ❧ I am connected to higher wisdom at all times.

I can't tell you how much saying these phrases out loud to myself several times a day, every day, impacted my life in a positive way. Not only did they help me to create my life, they also gave me a wonderful sense of empowerment. Try it for yourself. You will begin to feel like you can do anything! They also act as mental commands that sink into the deeper layers of your mental body. After repeating these affirmations enough times, they will become part of your subconscious mind, which is when they become part of your new neural net. One word of caution: don't try to figure out when your new neural net has finally taken hold. Instead, your best bet is to faithfully carry out the exercises every day, and to continue them, even after you start experiencing the amazing results that will most definitely occur. The best part about consistently saying these positive affirmations every day is that, in order to commit to this, you have to make the decision that you are worth it. That decision alone will shift the overall direction and pattern of your life.

≋ 33 ≋

Clearing the Physical Body

C LEARING YOUR PHYSICAL body is another vitally important step towards gaining total control over your Reality Creation and your power of manifestation. Any time you are attempting to manifest something in your life, your ability to do so will be dependent upon the strength of your energy field. If you are physically unfit or unhealthy in any way, your energy field is compromised. This is because: 1) When you have any sort of health concern, your body utilizes all available energy to heal itself; and 2) You will be mentally drawn to focus upon this area until you are healed. In other words, your ability to focus is hindered by the fact that you have a nagging concern that continuously draws your attention and energy away from your intended manifestation.

Healing and fine-tuning your physical body is a necessary step towards mastering the Art of Manifestation. You don't need to become a workout maniac, go on a crash diet or fast for 30 days. However, establishing a regular workout routine, having a balanced diet, and doing occasional cleanses is definitely recommended. Your body is the vehicle with which you experience your Reality Creation. If you think about it, it's the whole reason to manifest anything at all. If you manifest a new car, you need to be physically well enough to drive it, right? If you manifest a new house, you want to be healthy enough to be able to enjoy it. If you manifest your new dream job, you have to be able to perform optimally. If you now are able buy fantastic new clothes because your new dream job pays you tons of cash, you want to fit in them and look great, right? And, if you haven't found your dream mate or partner yet, you definitely want to feel that you are physically appealing when you do don't you? You bet you do, to all of the above.

I like the concept of *baby steps*. Baby steps are particularly important when it comes to improving your health and fitness. One of the reasons my personal training business was so successful was because I had my clients implement small, incremental changes over a long period of time, instead of bull-rushing them with a zillion things to do at once. Invariably, most people fall off the wagon at one point or another. My answer to that was to *not create a wagon*. If you never work out and are overwhelmed by the idea, then just start by taking a short walk in the morning or evening three days a week through the park or around your neighborhood. This will form the building blocks for the foundation of your health and well being, and will also bring a sense of empowerment that may have been long missing from your life.

Next, or if you already take walks, decide that you are going to cut out one unhealthy thing from your daily eating routine. Again, baby steps work best because they are less threatening to the part of your unconscious that has enjoyed its comfort zone for so many years. Add one healthy thing to your diet, as well. For example, you may wish to have one less slice of bread or cut out a desert item, but then also add a shot of wheatgrass or a side salad. Once you get used to doing without the first type of unhealthy food you've eliminated from your diet, you can cut out the next unhealthy food, and then the next. As you gradually shift yourself away from unhealthy foods and begin adding more healthy foods to your diet, you will find that you've naturally developed the eating patterns that truly support your ultimate health.

If you already have a good diet and get some exercise, you can begin to fine tune your body. For ultimate fitness, you will need an integration of physical training (cardio and weight training), as well as some sort of mind/body connection exercise. My recommendation for the average person is to make sure they get some form of physical exercise at least two days a week then implement mind/body exercise for another two days a week. Examples of mind/body exercise are yoga, Pilates, tai chi, and chi kung. My personal regimen is five days a week weight training, two days a week running in the mountains, and some chi kung every day. We humans are unique, multi-faceted, multi-dimensional beings, who have a variety of different needs. Before long, you will come to know the routine that works best for you.

Key Points

✓ Start small with your exercise routine; do not try to take it all on at once.

✓ Begin with changes that are sustainable. Do not set yourself up for failure with a routine that is unrealistic for you.

✓ Create steps towards achieving the health and fitness you want. I like the idea of structuring your health regimen in three-month increments, with gradual increases in your regimen each month until you have reached your ideal routine.

✓ If you are having trouble getting started, hire a personal trainer. Their primary job is to motivate and inspire you in a positive way. I highly recommend utilizing these professionals, as a good trainer can make all the difference in helping you to achieve your health and fitness goals.

✓ For more aggressive dietary recommendations and serious health concerns, I recommend reading Dr. Robert Young's *The PH Miracle*.

≋ 34 ≋

Biochemistry

C LEARING YOUR PHYSICAL body will also im-
prove your biochemistry. Healthy biochemistry is essential to maintaining your optimum
state of well being. Unfortunately, biochemical depression is something that has become very pervasive in
our modern day society. Biochemical depression can
develop from a variety of factors, but I have found three
that are very common. These are: too much coffee, stress,
and lack of sleep. Oftentimes, these three can come as a
package deal.

Biochemical depression and altered emotional states
of being can develop very subtly, without your conscious awareness that they are taking place. What happens is that you begin to get a bit caught up in your 1,001
things to do a day. This may lead you to begin drinking too much coffee, or not. Either way, you can end up
extremely stressed out at the end of the day. You start

waking up in the middle of the night and can't get back to sleep because you are thinking about the 1,001 things you have to do. This is the beginning of a very vicious cycle that begins to create a hormonal imbalance within your body. You can eventually become depressed, neurotic, and even glucose intolerant from this process.

The next step in this downward spiral is the accelerated degeneration of your body. It begins with some tightness in various parts of your body, perhaps your neck and shoulders or lower back. Then comes the aches and pains that appear in your wrists, forearms, knees, shoulders, and lower back. Soon, digestive problems in the afternoon lead to stagnation in your stomach and intestines. What follows is the inability to digest many different foods, especially starches and sugars. Now, every time you have a glass of juice or something with bread in it, you feel water weight gain. The water retention, if you are not able to get rid of it through exercise or diet, becomes fat. Soon you are starting to put on weight and have aches and pains on top of that. In the meantime, from lack of proper sleep and taking caffeine to keep you going, you have developed a small case of biochemical depression. Now you are on anti-depressants, which oftentimes cause further hormonal imbalances that inevitably lead to more water retention and more health problems.

The answer to this raging epidemic? Cut back on your caffeine, sugars, and starches. Execute the above-mentioned exercise and nutritional recommendations. Begin doing some breathing and meditation exercises in the evening before you go to bed. This will help you fall asleep, stay asleep, and also get a better quality of sleep. You may use the "So-Hum" mantra meditation at night to help you sleep and in the morning to help you maintain a peaceful state of well being throughout the day.

Section Four: The Process Of Manifestation

"When we study the universe as a whole, with it's millions of galaxies, we have reached the largest scale of space and time; and again, at that cosmic level, we discover that the universe is not static-it is expanding!
—The Tao of Physics

Fritjof Capra

⪦ 35 ⪧

The Road to Ultimate Power

T HE PROCESS OF understanding and mastering The Art of Manifestation is also the road to self empowerment, or ultimate power. Through this process, you will be able to redirect your energy to create and manifest whatever you want with your life. This process will take the guesswork out of manifestation and bring the power back to you. Your only dilemma will be in deciding what you want—the rest is easy.

≋ 36 ≋

Deciding What You Want

WITHOUT EXCEPTION, THE single most important step in the process of manifestation is deciding what you want. Over the years, as I have worked with people to help them create the life they want, I have become aware of the power of decision. For many of my clients, the only thing they really needed to do was to decide what it was they really wanted. Once they decided—POOF! Instantaneous manifestation! The Universe loves a made-up mind and will often deliver instantaneously when you do. The key here is to understand how difficult that may be for you. So many people have no idea what they truly want, so they just kind of bounce from job to job, relationship to relationship, or from one situation to the next, feeling helplessly lost. When you become more decisive in your approach to life, you get more done. When you become more decisive in your approach to manifestation, you always get what you want. When you definitively decide the direction you want your life to go, life gets easier.

What do you really want? I recommend taking some time to yourself and getting clear about what you really want. Sometimes it's as easy as making a list of the material items that you would like to have in your life. Easy enough. But don't you also want to live a more rewarding, creative, and passionate life, as well? My experience is that most people do. Most people are not creating their life exactly the way they want it because they have not made the firm decision to do so. This means that you want the change, but are unwilling to make the decision to take responsibility for that change. When you decide unequivocally upon the specific direction you want to go in, then you will also take the necessary actions to effect that change. However, there will be no change without your firm commitment via a real decision about what you want.

Simply stated, *you cannot manifest anything without really wanting it*. For example, when I was younger, I always wanted to make money. However, I hated taking on too much responsibility and enjoyed my freedom. These conflicting wants created a lot of strife for me because I wanted the good life, but was unwilling to take the responsibility of creating it. This manifested as my going through the process of getting hired at various high-paying jobs, only to get fired shortly thereafter. After being fired from close to 20 jobs (that's right 20!), I realized that something wasn't working for me. I began to realize that money was important to me, but what was more important was having my freedom. So I became a bartender, which worked out great! I made good money, maintained my freedom, didn't have to take on too much responsibility, and had fun, to boot. The lesson for me was in being truthful with myself about what I really wanted during that particular period of my life and then not going against it.

≋ 37 ≋

Honesty Is Always The Best Policy

I N ORDER TO know what you want, it's a good idea to be honest with yourself. Sometimes, all you really want is to make more money, which provides you with more choices. That's completely fine and always extremely rewarding. Everyone should have the opportunity to make as much money as they want—no exceptions. However, I often find that people want more than just to have enough money. People want the feeling of *achievement* and *fulfillment*. Most people want to feel as if they have completed something of value and they want to feel joy about what they do.

A good friend of mine is a medical doctor who had decided to take a hiatus from her work. While speaking with her on the telephone, I began to understand that she was really quite distraught about her career. She had called me from Kansas City, where she was staying for awhile. As she was talking about how much she loved visiting the art museum there, I couldn't help but notice that all of the stress and tension had left her voice; instead, she sounded enthusiastic and passionate. A thought came to my mind. "You know," I offered, "There's a theory that says the greatest success in life is what is closest to your heart." There was a pause on the other end of the line, and then she excitedly replied, "Wow, that makes a lot of sense!" I hadn't really said much, but I knew something had clicked for her.

As a result of that conversation, my friend came to the realization that she had *always* loved museums and artwork. She called me a short time later to tell me she had decided to pursue a career as a museum curator. I have never seen her happier. For her, the answer wasn't the high-pressure, high-paying job of being a doctor; it was following her passion of working with artwork and museums. I happen to think that becoming a doctor or healer is one of the most valuable things a person can do with their lives, but if you are pursuing a career only for the money, it may not be as rewarding or fulfilling.

In order to manifest something, anything at all, you need to know what you want. The Universe cannot deliver something to you if you are undecided about what you want. Conversely, if you decide to create something that you only partly want, meaning that you are not totally committed to it, it may take a long time to manifest. In the case of my doctor friend, she was forced to take a hiatus to try and figure out what she really wanted. A hiatus is good, but if you are forced to take one, it could be because you are doing something that you don't really want to be doing. If you are experiencing any of the signs and symptoms listed below, it could be an indication that your heart is not really in your current occupation:

- ✤ Chronic fatigue
- ✤ Depression
- ✤ Irritability
- ✤ Not making enough money
- ✤ Overcompensating on the weekends with heavy partying, internet gaming, drinking, gambling, drug abuse, or anything at all you find yourself doing obsessively.

For example, let's say you are a customer service specialist in an IT tech company and you've decided to manifest a management promotion; you may have some trouble manifesting this promotion if it's not what you *really* want. If what you really want is to be an independent music producer, you most likely will find that it takes you longer to manifest the IT management position. What happens here is that your growing desire to become an independent music producer will interfere with your desire to gain a management position in your company. This is because you have conflicting desires and are unclear about what you really want. Again, any sort of confusion or cloudiness about what you want will slow down or completely stop your manifestation. The confusion you experience when you are unclear about what you want in this moment serves to lower your vibrational rate of attraction. How excited do you feel about life when you are confused about what you want? Thus, the more clear you are about what you want *in this moment*, the quicker your manifestation time will be. Your Reality Creation will come to a screeching halt until you decide exactly what it is you want right *now*.

In this instance, if your burning desire is to own your own music production company, then that is what you need to focus on. State your intention out loud to the Universe. This way, you will begin to harness all of the available energy to utilize in the manifestation of your desire. When you are completely decided on what it is you want, you will be amazed at the short turnaround time.

≋ 38 ≋

Deciding What You Want Now Versus What You Want Later

BECAUSE MOST PEOPLE are unclear about where they want to wind up down the road and what they want to do with the rest of their lives, a great way to free up that energy is to let it go. Instead, decide what would be the most fun and beneficial to you right now in this moment. I like the concept of "segmenting" as introduced in the Abraham/Hicks book *Ask and It is Given*. Here, what you do is break up your life into smaller segments and decide how you want each segment to be.

It's okay if you do not know what you want to do with your whole life. Take the pressure off by thinking about what you would like to do *right now* instead. Not only does this take the pressure off your life, it also brings the fun and creativity back in. Also, it serves to release resistance to the present moment by allowing you to flow your energy freely again by focusing on what you want. I find it really invigorating to suddenly change gears, scrap the idea of thinking about what I need to do with the *rest of my life*, and instead just think about what I would like to do for the next couple of years. Doing this can provide you with the much-needed freedom to create yourself anew and give yourself a break from having to figure it all out right now.

≋ 39 ≋

The Difference Between "Shoulds" and "Wants"

ANOTHER AREA THAT may snag you up is the idea of thinking that there is something you *should* be doing. You *should* be doing only what you *want* to do. In other words, there is nothing you are supposed to be doing with your life. Stated another way, *you are only really doing what you are supposed to be doing when you are doing what you really want to be doing.* When you are doing what you really want to be doing, you are also closest to your heart center. Coincidentally, when you are close to your heart center, you are also the happiest and the most enthusiastic. In turn, you radiate more positive energy and uplift the people around you.

Many of my friends, including myself at one point, have struggled off and on with this concept in our lives. I used to sit and meditate all day, every day, on what I was *supposed* to be doing with my life. The only thing that happened was I accumulated more unpaid bills. That sucked. Eventually, I realized that I needed to decide upon the course of action I would take with my life. Even though I still didn't know what I ultimately wanted to do with my life, I decided to take action. As a result, I became more productive. The truth was, I enjoyed my life much more after I finally got off my butt and started moving in the direction of what I *wanted right now.*

Many spiritual seekers wander around asking themselves, *"What am I supposed to be doing?"* The idea that you are *supposed* to do something is what I would term a spiritual myth. I'm here to tell you, once and for all, that the only thing you *should* be doing is what you *want* to do. If you sit around and meditate about it all day, you're going to wind up depressed and broke. Often people have distorted ideas about spiritual freedom. "I just want to be free," is a common phrase, but many people do not understand what true freedom really means.

Unwittingly, many seekers misapply the concept of spiritual freedom to validate their victim consciousness. Total freedom looks completely different from sitting around broke with nothing to do except to meditate on being "spiritual." Total freedom comes from mastering every area of your life and giving yourself the choices to do or be whatever you want. I have met people who are, in my opinion, true spiritual masters. What sets them apart is not that they are superhuman or completely deprived of material items, but rather that they have mastered every area of their life. They have manifested abundance in their work, their finances, their emotional well being, their relationships, their mental faculties, and also their spiritual foundation. They are still human and can be vulnerable to negative thinking, but their lives are well-integrated and they are generally not unconsciously reactive. In other words, they are free from the idea of limitation.

⇛ 40 ⇚

Why Do You Want What You Want?

Y OUR NEXT STEP is to figure out *why* you want what you want. Doing this can help you to become more clear about what you really want—or if you even really want it at all. A lot of people say that they want to become rich and famous. I like to ask the question, *Why? Why do you want to become rich and famous?* Do you really have a true burning desire within you to be a superstar, or is it that you are trying to fill your missing sense of self with external validation? In my opinion, a great many people are trying to become something they are not. Each and every one of us is already a superstar waiting to manifest. It's more a matter of uncovering the superstar within yourself, rather than seeking something outside of you. Everyone deserves to have everything they want, but a lot of people confuse what they really want with unconscious motivation and childhood programming.

If you think about it, much of the struggle and strife in this world comes from the actions of people who are continually seeking external validation and approval, along with building up their ego image. These behaviors stem from unhealed emotional wounds which drive us to look outside of ourselves for a sense of meaning. Many of us end up working our butts off, trying to get someone's attention for approval. We may not even love what we do, but we are driven to succeed so that we can gain approval and validation. When you are doing what you are doing for external validation, it will always be a struggle, because no one can ever give you enough validation. When you are doing what you are doing because you love it, the activity or job will seem easy and perhaps even effortless.

Once in awhile, your search for external validation can lead you to stumble across a career path or business idea that really does provide you with a sense of self. However, this is usually only the case because you already *know* yourself, have done the work, and have become magnetic to something that represents who you are.

It is okay to want something because you need to prove to yourself that you can do it or attain it. This behavior is only unhealthy when you are doing it to prove to others that you can do it or attain it. In this case, you are striving for external validation as the meaning of your existence. Even after you achieve it, you will still feel something missing inside of you. On top of that, you will have expended tons of energy trying to prove to or impress other people that you are good enough.

Another reason you may not be clear about what you really want is that you might be attempting to manifest something out of fear. You may be fearful that you will not be able to make a living in your desired occupation or that you will never find a mate who truly loves and respects you. So you have a bit of poverty consciousness, or a belief in limitation of some sort, that says you need to take what you can get. If the bills are due now, and I mean right now, then your first manifestation will need to be getting the bills paid. However, if your bills are paid right now, but you're scared that you won't be able to pay them in the future, then it is time to let go of the fear. Instead, create out of your desire to express yourself and become something more. Create out of the joy and passion of redefining yourself and becoming more than you have ever been. Your ability to do this will open you up to a completely new perspective from which you will view the world.

If you are attempting to create a relationship out of the fear of being alone, you could also refer to this at a type of poverty consciousness. Again, poverty consciousness is the belief in limitation, that there is not enough. It is impossible for someone else to get or have the resources that are available for you. Thus, there are plenty of available partners out there for you. However, your belief in limitation will cause you to reach for the first available one without even getting clear on what you want. It's true that nobody wants to be alone, but the difference is creating from a space of wanting versus a fear-based space of needing. If you are able to take the time to get clear about what you want before you jump into a relationship, you can become magnetic to a higher version of yourself. You will be consciously and purposefully creating your reality.

For example, you might say that you wanted a person who loves to mountain bike, tango dance, and cuddle up on the couch to watch movies on Sundays. You might also add that you want someone who has a great sense of humor and loves to laugh at everything in life. Conversely, you might want someone who is more serious minded who will take your requests seriously and pay more attention to your requests within the relationship. There is no wrong thing to want, only conscious and unconscious wanting or needing. If you take the time to figure out what you want and create the space necessary to consciously manifest it then you will be rewarded with exactly what you want.

If you are creating from a place of fear, you will never truly create exactly what you want. It's kind of like putting off your dreams to keep yourself safe. As I said before, "Behind every fear there lays a reward." Truly, every time I have ever moved through my fear, there has been a great reward waiting on the other side. Sometimes, in order to create what you really want, you will need to confront your deepest fears. It may even mean taking chances. All of the most successful people in the world became successful because they were willing to take chances.

≋ 41 ≋

Deserving and Worthiness

YOU MAY BE scared to actually declare what you truly want. In my experience, the biggest single emotional wound that most people have in common is the "deserving and worthiness" issue. Almost everyone I've ever met or worked with has had deserving and worthiness issues to one degree or another.

I had a client who worked through this issue in a very inspiring way. Jeff was a really great guy. Unfortunately, he had been a dot-com superstar who lost out on nearly everything in the late nineties. He lived with his lovely wife and three daughters in the Oakland Hills of California. Even though he couldn't really afford it, Jeff decided to hire me for in-home personal fitness training. The menial job he had when I met him barely paid the bills; the only thing he had going for him was that he and his wife already fully owned their home.

As I talked to Jeff throughout our sessions together, I began to get a sense of him. It wasn't that he couldn't get a job that paid more money, it was that he didn't feel worthy. Even his posture was slightly bent forward and he looked downwards when talking to people, as if he were a broken man. I had been training him for a few weeks, while at the same time telling him about the power of manifestation. Jeff was always visibly excited when I talked to him about the ability to create whatever you want in your life. On top of that, I noticed that as he put on a little muscle and lost a little body fat, he was gaining confidence. He was literally feeling more worthy and deserving of being who he was and breathing the air around him.

One day Jeff told me that he would not be able to continue training because he just couldn't afford it. He was beginning to feel badly about the fact that he was spending money on himself for personal training while he didn't have a lot of money to spend on his family. I told him this was completely understandable, but I also posed the question, "How much more money do you need to make?"

Jeff paused for a moment and I could tell that he sensed something important was about to happen. He looked at me and sort of mumbled, "Well, I don't know, probably about 75% more."

"Okay Jeff," I urged him, "Now say it like you mean it. I'll ask you again. How much more money do you want to make?!"

Jeff repeated his answer, a little more boldly, but still unsure of himself.

"Jeff," I said, "This is it. Do you want to make 75% percent more than what you are earning now, or not?"

Jeff was incredulous but excited at the same time. "Yes, yes I do." He was gaining confidence now.

"Good," I said. "So tell me what you want like you *mean* it!"

"I WANT A JOB THAT PAYS 75% MORE THAN I MAKE NOW!" There was strength in Jeff's voice and he was smiling from ear to ear.

Three days later I received a phone call from Jeff; he was excited and barely able to contain himself. "You won't believe it! My neighbor had a friend who was looking for someone to fill a position at their firm, and you'll NEVER guess how much it pays…!? It pays 75% more than what I make and they want *me* to work there!"

Three weeks later he had secured his position at the new job and began making exactly 75% more than his previous job had paid him. In this case, the Universe had simply been waiting for Jeff to realize that he was worthy enough to have what he really wanted. That may be all it takes for you, as well. When you are able to grasp that you were born worthy and deserving of experiencing whatever you want, then you will manifest it in your life.

≋ 42 ≋

Getting Clear About What You Want

S OMETIMES, IT'S A matter of putting all the pieces together so that you can clearly see what you want and why you want it, so that you can effectively clear yourself of any issues that may be holding you back from manifesting your heart's desire.

Getting clear about what you want

- ❧ No matter what, the single best exercise for getting clear on what you want is by making a list on a piece of paper. This will assist the manifestation process and sift through any mental clutter. Remember, include EVERYTHING that you want, you don't have to justify or rationalize anything to anyone.

- Decide what it is that you really want right now versus what you want later. I like the idea of two to three year segments in your life. When you do this, it will speed up your manifestation and take the pressure off of your decision-making process.

- It's okay if you do not know what you want to do for the rest of your life or where you want to wind up in ten years. Again, take the pressure off and instead just decide what you want to do *right now*. In other words, what is most important to you in this moment? Have fun with it and completely reinvent yourself if you like.

- Figure out why you want what you want. What is behind your driving desire or need to experience this outcome? If it's more money, then why? If it's a new career, then why? If it's a new partner or mate, why? There is no right or wrong answer here.

- After you figure out why you want what you want, write it down. If you can't think of a good enough reason to want it, you won't manifest it. In other words, if you want a new car, but you can't justify getting it, then this exercise will help you to identify that. It will help you to understand if you are not feeling deserving or worthy of having what you want, or if you are creating from a place of fear.

- Now, write down how having each of these items or manifested outcomes in your life will make you feel. How will it enhance your life and bring you joy? Be very descriptive, include both emotional feelings and physical feelings as well.

❧ Take a moment to see if you can feel what it's like to have the things on your list already manifested. You get into the feeling place of it by completely visualizing yourself in the desired circumstance as if you have already manifested it. What textures do you feel, what do you smell, what do you see, and how does it feel to have this thing?

≋ 43 ≋

Getting Clear About the
Relationship You Want

VIBRATIONALLY SPEAKING, RELATIONSHIPS have the ability to show us exactly where our vibrational rate of attraction is. You will never get a clearer picture of what you are attracting to yourself via your unconscious beliefs and emotional wounds than when you are in a relationship. This is your biggest mirror and the most primary indicator of where you are in your conscious awareness of self. Your partner will show you where your areas of greatest resistance lie. They will also show you what level of consciousness you are attracting to yourself. Your outer experience is always only a reflection of your inner beliefs and emotional wounds, likes and dislikes. When you consider the people you have chosen for relationships thus far, you may feel that you met them through a chance encounter, or that it was purely physical attraction that drew you together. But if you look a little deeper, you will no doubt recognize certain repeating patterns in your relationships; this is the indication that something in your psyche, or energy field, was a deciding factor in drawing the two of you together.

Most people do not take the time out between relationships, or, indeed, at all, to decide and list all of the things that they want in a partner. It may somehow feel impersonal to, in essence, create a person on a piece of paper. And yet, this is the single greatest thing you could do for yourself when it comes to attracting a life partner. When you do this, you are clearly saying that it is YOU who will choose the person you will be spending your life with. What is meant here is that you—not your emotional wounds and limiting unconscious beliefs—will be the deciding factor. Think about it, would *you* rather choose or have your emotional wounds choose for you? You cannot stop sending out your own unique signal to the Universe. And, since you are always broadcasting whether you like it or not, you might as well tailor the signal to meet your highest expectations rather than allowing it to broadcast from the default mechanism inside you.

Some confusion may arise at first when you sit down to do this great thing. The confusion usually arises from the realization that you may have never *truly* committed to finding the One. As an example, I have noted amongst many of my clients and friends that the most successful matchmaking companies are the ones that charge the most money. Now, I'm talking thousands of dollars here.

Also, what I'm not talking about is one of those high-society-rich-people-only dating networks. What I am referring to are the more serious and spiritually minded types of companies that make you commit to their program via a substantial monetary payment. Many people may scoff at the idea of paying a large sum of money to meet someone special and feel there is something inherently wrong with the idea. However, as I have observed thus far, a higher degree of committed and long lasting relationships result from these endeavors. Why is this? I'll tell you exactly why; it is because committing to that large a sum of money is committing to finding the One. In other words, suddenly being asked to put down a few thousand dollars will, at the very least, separate those people who are just kind of dating around from those people who really want to meet their life partner.

Similarly, I have found many people have a certain amount of resistance to the act of writing down what they want in a partner. *You have to believe that you are worth having everything you want out of a life partnership, as well. You have to believe that the Universe is limitless in its capacity to deliver what you want. You have to believe that as you write down what you want, you are in the process of changing the signal that you are putting out into the Universe.* You can't write it down without it affecting your vibrational rate of attraction, that's impossible. Conversely, you may find a certain amount of resistance to doing this if you feel that you are either unready for or undeserving of such a relationship.

You may already be in a relationship. By now you may be feeling that things are not exactly the way you want them to be, so much so that you are not sure this person is your life partner. My opinion is that any person can be your life partner; it is more a matter of how much resistance there is in your day-to-day existence with them. Generally speaking, if there is weekly or daily strife within your relationship, then it is time to take a look. If, while still in your relationship, you were to do the exercise of writing down everything you want in your life partnership, you would find one of two things happening: A) This person would begin to actually transform; or B) This person would fade away from your reality so that your true partner could arrive. It can be terrifying to think about, especially if you really, really want the person you have now to be the One. However, severe attachment is not coming from your Higher Self, but rather from your lower self. Only your lower self believes in limitation, abandonment, and all of the things that would keep you tethered to something that does not serve your highest good.

If you are in a relationship that is almost, but not quite what you want and you undertake exercises that will elevate your vibrational rate of attraction, change will become inevitable. *You simply have to believe that you are actually and truly worthy of having someone who honors your highest good as you would theirs. Everyone is worthy of this, it is simply a matter of recognizing and claiming it.* You cannot change the other person, but you can elevate your own vibrational rate of attraction.

Doing so will always serve your highest good. Indeed, doing this is the single greatest gift you can give yourself. You will become magnetic to a higher vibrational circle of people. There is no judgment, again, only what serves your highest good and what does not. Every step of conscious awareness serves the purpose of further learning and teaching and change is only necessary if you are not happy where you are. Isn't it worth it to give your present or future relationship the best possible opportunity to truly fulfill your highest good?

≋ 44 ≋

The Power of Wanting vs. Yearning

BEFORE WE GO any further, I'd like to clarify the difference between "wanting" something, as opposed to "yearning" for it. Traditionally, to be in a constant state of wanting is to never be happy with what you have or where you are. In this state you are never in the Now, you are always in the future somewhere. As your point of power is Now, in this moment, it is in your best interest to understand what genuine wanting really is. A genuine want is an expectant feeling of having something that appeals to you. This means that you, in your wanting of it, *know you can attain it*. You may conceive that it will require a lot of work ahead to achieve it, or very little. Regardless, you are experiencing a state of joy as you think of this thing because you are genuinely wanting it. Energetically, this state of joy has a higher vibration, which actually serves to attract the thing you are wanting into your life.

What you are not doing, however, is to wish you had this thing or circumstance, all the while knowing that you never will. This is called *yearning*. If you find yourself observing something you want, and at the same time feeling negatively about the possibility of it ever coming to you, you are in a state of yearning. In this state, you are the farthest from genuine wanting that you could possibly be. Here you are disallowing the flow of your own energy by not believing that you could ever achieve or have this thing in your life. This stems from the frustration and pain of not allowing yourself to do, be, or have what you want in your life.

When you really want something, in a genuine, unimpeded way, it's very exciting. You feel pumped at the prospect of eventually attaining this thing or achieving the goal. When you are yearning for something, there is only the disempowering feeling of wanting something that you know you will never have. Generally speaking, yearning is a great way to block all of the good that can come to you. The reason for this is that you are emitting a lower vibrational energy field while in the process of observing something that you want. In other words, you are repelling the outcome that you want with a vibrational energetic field that does not match it.

Conversely, when you declare that you want something with excitement and enthusiasm, it is already on the way. The vibrational dynamics of the Universe are such that you have set your manifestation power in motion. The Universe always delivers what you think about and believe in. When you genuinely want something, you are also believing that you can have it.

So let's say that you are ready to meet your soulmate. I mean, you are *really* ready. You've been reading all kinds of soulmate books on attracting the one and you're all fired up! You are, in this moment, genuinely wanting a soulmate. You're excited about it, which means that you are also probably having some visual images about it, as well. It's exciting, because in this state of genuine wanting, you know this person is now on the way. So, you head out to the bookstore, pick out a magazine, and sit down to start reading. Looking up, you notice a cute couple sitting across from you, all lovey-dovey, cuddled up next to each other reading. Here is where a problem could arise; for some reason it doesn't feel good to see these people so in love. It's a bit of an irony, you might say, because they have what you want. And yet, you are definitely not feeling positive about seeing these people involved in what you want to be involved in, doing what you would like to be doing. Why is this?

In this moment, you have fallen prey to the feeling of yearning. What happens here is a chain reaction. Your first impression is seeing something that you want. What quickly follows, however, is that you observe this thing to be outside of yourself. Meaning, you perceive this thing or event as not being yours to have—it is someone else's. Unfortunately, since you have been wanting this thing for so long, you have begun to believe that you will *never* have it. Thus, seeing someone else having something you want, something you believe you cannot have, becomes painful. After the feeling of yearning, you may begin to experience other, even more negative, feelings and emotions. You may actually start to judge other people for having what you want. Then you may begin to resent them from feeling as if they have a better life than you do. You may even begin to feel anger towards them for getting to experience what you wish to experience. Now, in this moment, you have completely forgotten about your genuine want of having your own soulmate in your own life.

The key here, then, is to embrace seeing the thing you want, whenever you see it. It doesn't matter where you see it, who has it, or how much it costs. Your only objective is to embrace it by getting excited about it. Praise God or the Universe for creating it so that you could know it even existed! It took me some practice to master this. Because there were so many things I wanted that I hadn't allowed myself to have, whenever I actually saw someone else who had it, the experience was challenging, to say the least. Also, being raised by a family who had poverty consciousness as a way of life, I always wanted to have money. Some money, any money at all would do, thank you very much! Creating a wonderful, rewarding, and harmonious intimate relationship was also important to me. After wanting these things for so long enough without getting them, I got tired of seeing them in other people's lives. It became even more painful as my genuine wanting turned into yearning. For a long while, I was unable to get past this concept, so I continued avoiding situations where I would be forced to be around people who had what I wanted. I didn't want them to see or feel my negativity and I didn't want to pretend that I was happy that they had what I didn't. Intellectually, I understood the difference between yearning and genuine wanting, but I just couldn't seem to get past my strong feelings of resentment.

Then one day I decided to really try it out. I remember sitting in front of a BMW dealership and admiring a new BMW. It was a brand new M3 convertible with custom racing rims—I think they were like 19's. It was sweet! I felt that old emotional energy of yearning in the background begin to well up and take over. Instead of letting it win out, I began to purposefully admire this amazing car in front of me. I visualized myself in it, driving it down Santa Monica Boulevard. I felt happiness and joy at its mere existence. I felt gratitude towards the makers of BMW for inventing this amazing machine. Now, this was a step in the right direction. I didn't quite manifest the M3, but I did manifest a brand new 330ci BMW. I still catch myself yearning for something occasionally, but I am usually able to pretty quickly redirect myself into the positive emotion of genuine wanting.

≡ *45* ≡

Healing Unconscious Sabotage Mechanisms and Beliefs

T HE BEST WAY to identify any unconscious beliefs and sabotage mechanisms that may be blocking you from successful manifestation is to use your want list. You can use this list to pinpoint any unconscious resistance you may be experiencing and heal it, thus opening the way for you to manifest the items on your list.

Healing Unconscious Sabotage Mechanisms and Beliefs

- ⤳ First, either use your existing list of wants or write down a list of wants. The best way to do this exercise is to be as free as possible with the things you include on your list. Be completely unrealistic, make this list completely outlandish.

This is not the place for your inner critic or censor; this *is* the place for your inner artist or inner child to go crazy and have fun.

- Next, next to each item, event, thing, or scenario on your list, write down why you can't have it. Figure out a reason why you should not be able to have this thing. If you can't find a reason, then you should already have this thing or be able to manifest it pretty quickly. Write down at least one reason per item on your list.

- From this point, take each reason why you can't have the item on your list and write down the exact opposite of it. For example, if you wanted to manifest your soulmate or life partner, and your reason for not having them in your life was that you felt you were not worthy, write down now that you *are* worthy. This is a challenging exercise, so be prepared for what comes up. It could be that what comes up next is that you feel like you are unready. If this feels right, then you will know by the good feeling you get by deciding to wait awhile. If it doesn't feel good and you still feel like you want to have your Soulmate *now*, then continue writing down more reasons why you can't have this. If you ever can't figure out a reason why you can't have something, then point blank ask yourself, *Why can't I have it?* The answer will always come.

- When things come up, like "I'm not worthy" or "It's not time yet," that's great! Now you *know* why you don't have your life partner yet. Knowledge is power, so now you get to either decide that you are not ready or decide that you are ready and write it down. For every reason you come up with for why you cannot have something, write down the exact opposite reason for why you can.

- In this manner you will discover many, if not all of the unconscious beliefs and sabotage mechanisms that keep you from creating what you want. From that point, you get to decide if it's a good enough reason to not create it or have it. If, for example, you decide that you are not ready for some big thing or event, it may be that you are really unprepared and need some time. Now you have become conscious of your unconscious and are in a more powerful position to create what you want.

- Going down your list of wants in this way will quickly establish why you don't have all of the things that you want in your life. Each time you rewrite a reason for not having it into a reason for having it, you are reprogramming your neural network. Each time you do this you are bringing yourself closer to having the desired outcome.

- You can continue on and go further with this exercise for what you may feel are bigger, more challenging manifestations. Say you want to become the CEO of your company and you are presently only a customer service representative.

You may find many reasons why you can't have the CEO position in your company. And yet, as you do the exercise of rewriting all the reasons you can't have this position into reasons why you can, you will be amazed at the changes that happen in your life. You will witness unexplainable synchronicities and changed attitudes and behaviors around you and towards you, all leading you to the desired position. This is an excellent technique for uncovering a great deal of the unconscious beliefs or motivations behind why you do what you do and changing them all into desired outcomes.

❧ Here is an example of how you go about this exercise:

My want:	I want a Lamborghini Marcielago.
Reason can't have it:	It is way too expensive and unrealistic.
Reason can have it:	For me it's affordable, cheap, and easily manageable.
Reason can't have it:	It eats up too much gas.
Reason can have it:	There is plenty of gas for everyone. When there is not, we will invent way cooler cars that run on alternative energy sources.
Reason can't have it:	I don't have a place to park it!

Reason can have it:	When I get my new Lamborghini I will park it in my new house.
Reason can't have it:	I can't afford the insurance.
Reason can have it:	The insurance is easily affordable, especially with this amazing business deal that I just made.
Reason can't have it:	It's just too ridiculous and unrealistic for cryin' out loud!
Reason can have it:	I don't play by the rules which means that I get to achieve all of my dreams!

⤚ If you are continuing to feel any emotional discomfort or inner conflict as you do this exercise, simply use this deserving and worthiness release to clear yourself of any emotional blockages that may be connected to these belief systems.

Deserving and Worthiness Emotional Release

⤚ Say out loud to yourself, "I am unworthy and undeserving of the life that I want."

⤚ Now, see if you can allow yourself to feel this as fully as you can. This is only a temporary exercise, so it's ok to allow yourself to feel this for a second. If it brings up bad feelings then realize it's only because at some level you actually believe it. This is good, now we know. If it doesn't bring anything up, then you do not believe it and will remain completely unaffected.

- Next, ask yourself, "Could I release this feeling?"
- Give yourself at least a full minute to just be with this question.
- Now, see how you are feeling.
- Say out loud the opposite, "I am worthy and deserving of the life that I want."
- Now, see what feelings that this statement brings up.
- Now, see if you can allow yourself to either feel the positive or negative feelings that may come up.
- Ask yourself if you could release these emotions. You may be thinking, but I don't want to release *good feelings*! It's ok, you can't release good feelings, you will only be releasing the illusion that you have to deserve or be worth something.
- Take a second to be with the question.

Releasing both ways is powerful. Continue this exercise until it feels good to state what you want out loud.

≋ 46 ≋

Allowing It to Happen

T HE NEXT STEP can be difficult, but it is a vital component to the process of manifestation: *Allow your manifestation to happen in its own time and in its own way.* Strictly speaking, this part of the process has nothing to do with you and everything to do with the mechanics of the Universe. When you put the energy of creation, through thought, out into the Universe, with the intention of manifesting a specific outcome, the only thing left to do is to allow the Universe to deliver.

A common question asked by many people is, "Why hasn't it happened yet?" The answer to that question is almost always, "Because you haven't *allowed* it to happen yet." It's hard to just state your intention and then let it go. Oftentimes, there is a lot of hoping and wishing that completely contradicts and cancels out this process. If you hope and wish for something, then you aren't really believing you can create whatever you want. Everyone was born with this ability, so it makes no sense to hope for something that is already yours. The only thing you really need is to learn how to harness this power to purposefully create the life that you want. And besides, proper prayer is not begging for something, it is affirming it and knowing it. You do not need to beg or plead for what is already yours. You merely need to get clear on what it is that you want, state your intention to manifest it, then allow the Universe to deliver it to you in its own way.

≡ 47 ≡

Realize That You Are Worth It

I FEEL LIKE it's important to cover the issue of worthiness again when it comes to the *allowing* step. Many religions teach that you must *earn* God's love, that until you do you are not worthy. This creates the tendency to use what I refer to as "false prayer." Again, I must say that I have gone through periods in my own life where I begged and pleaded with God and the Universe for things to happen and change in my life. However, I only did so because I did not realize that you don't have to earn the right to have whatever you want. You only need to believe in yourself and know that you are worthy.

Every single person in the world is worthy of asking for what they want. Again, proper asking is doing so not out of fear or a sense of lack, but out of a sense of empowerment, excitement, and enthusiasm for having what you really want. For people in difficult situations, this can be challenging. There may be a feeling of deserving to be punished or doing penance for a previous misdeed. This belief is only so because you have made it so. Sometimes we feel as if we must help someone or be entrained to them because they helped us in some way. In this case, you are feeling unworthy of creating for yourself and instead you must create for this other person first because they helped you. An example of this may be the feeling that you owe somebody for being there for you. Perhaps they helped support you through college so now you are taking care of them financially for the next four years. To a certain degree, this may feel rewarding and also feel like the right thing to do. However, if years later in your life you find yourself still answering to this person and building your life around their wants and needs, then you might be doing it from a place of obligation. You should really only help someone if it feels good to do so. If you are helping someone begrudgingly, then you are lowering your vibrational energy field. If it's something that you really feel you need to do, then accept it and move on. If you are doing it out of your unconscious obligation issues, then it may be time to break out of this cycle. Use your feeling power to discern the best course of action for you in any circumstance.

You do not need to prove you are worthy of anything. If you are a human being, then you were born worthy and deserving of creating whatever you want. Feel free to manifest your heart's desire. If you find it difficult to suddenly believe that you are completely worthy and deserving of creating whatever you want, then take baby steps. If you just can't get yourself to believe that you are worthy, work on manifesting smaller goals in your life. For example, going back to Jeff and his amazing 75% manifestation, if I had pushed Jeff to attempt to manifest a job that paid 150% more than what he was currently making instead of only 75% more, I may have encountered resistance. At that time, it took him all he could muster to believe that he was actually worthy of a job that paid 75% more. However, this was still an amazing accomplishment for him. So, instead of pushing him into unknown territory, I allowed *him* to choose how much more money he *felt* like he was worth making.

If you want to make a whole lot of money, you may wish to build up your belief system of deservingness and worthiness by starting with something that is a push for you, but not so completely unimaginable that you will never manifest it. If you are only making $60,000 a year at this moment, but want to one day make $1,000,000 a year, it might benefit you to begin building up your belief in your ability to manifest. Now, anyone, and I mean ANYONE, can manifest anything at any time with the right mental, emotional, and spiritual precision. However, in this case, it might benefit you to first shoot for a six-figure income. After you achieve that, you will have built up your belief in your ability to manifest, as well as your feeling of worthiness for having more money.

≋ 48 ≋

The Fallacy of Karmic Retribution

NOTHER BELIEF THAT may tie you up is the idea of *karma*. It's a fact that karma exists, but it is not this dangerous entity that is out to get you. Rather, karma is an impersonal facet of the mechanics of the Universe and is run on an automated system. It is as simple as action-reaction. You put something out to the Universe, you get it back. You swerve in front of someone in traffic, two miles down the road someone swerves in front of you. You rob an old woman when you're 15 years old, you get robbed when your 50. You're nice to a homeless person and give them some money, the next day you pick up a new client for your business. You help someone change a tire, down the road someone helps you change yours. Karma is constantly in effect, whether we know it or not, whether we like it or not. It is not good or bad, it simply exists. Humans are the only creatures that have ever put any kind of judgment on karma.

Where does it come from? Well, where does anything come from? My theory is that God created Karma to help us learn, grow, and become responsible for our actions. As a completely automated, impersonal system, karma exists as a facet of quantum mechanics. As we take an action, speak a word, or have a thought, we are sending out energetic waves into the Universe. These waves are magnetic to like waves, group with them, and then return to their source or origin, which is you. This is yet another reason to take full responsibility for your thoughts, words, and actions. If you feel like you have been sending out negative energy waves to the Universe, do not be quick to blame yourself. Instead, take responsibility for what you're putting out by deciding that you are going to put out energy that you would like to receive yourself one day. In this manner, you will begin to consciously create your own karma. Wow, what an amazing concept!

I know many spiritual seekers who will readily proclaim that they are suffering this thing or that thing as a result of their past-life karma. This is a great way to externalize your power and make yourself completely helpless. How does it help you to suffer at the hands of your past lifetime experience? You create your own reality in this moment, here now. At any time, you can decide that you are done suffering and begin to affect your vibrational field with new positive thoughts about who you are and what you want to experience in this lifetime. In your conscious realization of your power in this moment, you will harness all the forces of the Universe to create what you want.

There is definitely some merit to past-life experiences, but the only real practicality is in absolving chronic issues. In other words, you may be creating your reality from a place of victim consciousness, based on a situation in your life that you feel is the result of your past-life karma; this is completely unnecessary and wholly your creation. However, seeking out a good hypnotherapist to take you through a past life regression so that you can re-experience an issue from your Higher Self perspective can be productive. Great examples of this can be found in the books by Brian Weiss, M.D. and Dr. Michael Newton. Occasionally, there is some sort of real malady that someone can actually release and absolve through past-life regression therapy. However, most people do not have anything from their past lives blocking their creative freedom in this one. If you have given any power away to this idea, I strongly suggest that you scrap it immediately and get back to the here and now. I liken it to tying an imaginary anchor onto your ankle and then dragging yourself around as if its real. That's not much fun, if you ask me. Perhaps it's time to untie this imaginary thing and get back to enjoying your life.

If you are really that concerned about karma, then build up a positive karmic bank account. A great way to do this is to help people, when and if you can. Donate to your favorite charity if you have an overabundance of money. Give silent blessings to the people around you. Stay calm in traffic and smile more. Become a positive inspiration for all of your friends and family. It will all come back to you, it always does.

≋ 49 ≋

Detachment from Outcome

S o much can be said about achieving detachment from the outcome of your efforts. When you are totally detached from the outcome of your intended manifestation, you can then allow it to manifest in its own time and in its own way. People who have mastered the ability to completely detach from the outcome of their intended manifestations enjoy 100% turnaround. In other words, every time they intend to manifest something, they get it.

What quantum physicists have found out is that when a human being focuses their attention upon something, they are actually freezing it in space/time. Not only that, but your attention will fix it in place and expand it. In other words, when you dwell upon a particular thought, whether it be something helpful or harmful to your well being, you will expand that thought in your consciousness. As you expand that thought in your consciousness, you become magnetic to the emotional charge that particular thought or line of thinking is creating for you.

As an example, if you are between jobs and over your ears in debt, you will have much difficulty if you cannot detach from the idea of your debt. Now, occasionally someone can use their tough circumstance to suddenly pull themselves up by their bootstraps and overcome the odds. However, what people generally do is to focus with growing concern upon their debt and unpaid bills. It only makes good sense, right? I mean, you have to be responsible, which means you can't just forget about your debt. Or can you?

When you focus upon your debt, unpaid bills, lack of good health, etc., you are, in effect, expanding these problems in your consciousness and becoming magnetic to more of the same. You will need to detach from the unpaid bills, the lack of good health, or any other concern that you have for the moment. If you do not, it will continue to grow in your experience until it becomes overwhelming. Sometimes, this is a difficult lesson that a person must learn, no matter how unfortunate it may appear. However, as far as the mechanics of manifestation are concerned, it is always avoidable.

≋ 50 ≋

Focus Upon What You Want, Not
What You Don't Want

B Y FAR, ONE of the greatest lessons I have ever learned about manifestation is to focus upon what you want, not what you don't want. This is the quickest way to get rid of your unpaid bills, debts, health concerns, and anything else you don't want in your life. It's pretty easy, just think about all the things you don't want and write down the opposite of each one. If you don't want debt, then you must want abundance. If you don't want bad health, you must want to be healthy and vital. If you don't want to argue with your mate all the time, you must want a happy, harmonious relationship. If you don't want a used beat up old car, you must want a shiny new one in perfect condition. If you don't want to be confused, unhappy, and lost, you must want to be confident, upbeat, and on track. This is also a super way of getting started on your manifestation process.

A Different Way to Figure Out What You Want

- ✤ Sit down and create a list of all the things you don't want to experience.

- ✤ Now, write down the opposite of each item on the list. Sometimes it is better to write down something that symbolizes the opposite. Again, a great example is debt and unpaid bills. What you want is to have them all paid, once and for all, right? The problem is, if you write down "no debt and no bills" your attention and energy is still focused upon debt and bills. The Universe doesn't get from that "no more unpaid bills," the Universe gets "more unpaid bills please." You have to be careful where your focal point really is when you want to manifest, and, for that matter, even when you don't. You are always putting out a signal, emitting your personal energetic magnetism to the Universe. So, it's always better to be in control of what you're putting out so you can reap the rewards of a purposefully- constructed life.

- ✤ How do you reword "no more unpaid bills" into something constructive that symbolizes "no more unpaid bills?" You visualize what having no more unpaid bills might look like. If you had no more unpaid bills and no more debt, what would that represent to you? Where would you be and what would you be doing? I doubt very much that you would be doing exactly what you're doing right now. You might be, though—you might just be sitting at home, relaxing in the ease and comfort of *The Magical Land of No Bills or Debt.* Most people would probably be taking a big vacation or a break somewhere. In other words, what you really want to do is visualize yourself somewhere above and beyond the mere opposite of where you want to be.

❧ In this case, visualize yourself with *extra* money to spend. You want to completely take your focus off of the unpaid bills and debt. You do this by visualizing what you would do with extra money. This completely detaches you from the idea of debt and puts your focus on the idea of abundance.

For example, at one point in my life I was in serious debt. This is actually untrue—at *many* points in my life I was in debt, it just so happened that at this particular point I was ready to put my manifestation skills to the ultimate test. The test was this: Either I was going to become homeless or else I was going to get some income rolling in. Well, I chose to get some income rolling in. I was three car payments behind, past due by 20 days on my rent, had bill collectors calling me every hour on the hour—things were not looking good. Fortunately, I was able to remember NOT TO FOCUS on everything going on around me at that moment. *I had to keep my focus on what I wanted, not what I didn't want. In this way I could detach from the unpaid bills and debt, and release them to allow abundance back into my life.*

I decided the best thing to do was to just pick one thing to focus on that was not so challenging I wouldn't believe it and thereby block my manifestation with doubt. I understood that when you are down in the trenches, you cannot challenge yourself with something that will seem too unbelievable. Further, if I attempted to focus upon something too extreme (like a million dollars) I would create resistance for myself. Instead of trying to manifest money to pay my bills, which I knew would only be depressing, I visualized my email account full of requests from new clients wanting to sign up for training. Not only did I visualize my email chalk full, but I was actually able to feel the excitement of going to my email, opening it up, and then seeing 20 emails from new prospective clients.

Now, what I wanted to do right away was go and check my email to see if it worked. Bad idea. I ran upstairs, got online, checked my email, and got zippo. I was frustrated, but a little voice in the back of my mind said, "Remember, you need to detach and allow this to happen." So I calmed down and told myself to relax. I then made a deal with myself to only check my email once a day in the evening at 9 pm. This way, I would completely detach from the outcome and allow the Universe to deliver my new clients to me. I remembered what one of my teachers had said to me some years ago, "When you put the bread in the oven, does it bake any faster if you open the oven and check on it every 30 seconds? Or, does it actually slow down the process and end up taking more time?" Now I had it. I waited a whole day to check my email again. In the meantime, I read a good book so that I would completely let go and allow my manifestation to take place.

The next night I checked my email. *PRESTO!* A new client had emailed me. I was excited, but this was just one client and I hadn't even booked them yet. I realized that I still needed to stay calm and remember to continue visualizing my email inbox full of new clients. So I did and waited until the next night at 9 pm to check again. This time THREE new clients had contacted me! Incredible! Now I was rolling again. I continued to only check my email once a day, while two to three times a day I visualized my email account full of clients. It worked like a charm and inside of three weeks I was booked solid! This was my first great lesson in detachment and how easy it is to manifest something when you are completely detached from the outcome.

It's such a simple concept: The art of detachment through focusing upon what you want, not what you don't want. If you master the ability to do this, your life will take on a magical quality. The people I know who are able to practice this art every day lead the most incredible lives you've ever heard of. They are always joyous, happy, and free. This is not an exaggeration. I used to wonder how the heck it was that these people always seemed to be on vacation somewhere while I toiled and struggled in my day-to-day existence. On top of that, they all had a bigger monthly nut than I did—I mean, a lot bigger! They all had nice homes, plenty of material items, great relationships, and were constantly on vacation. I just couldn't get it, until I finally did. They all had one thing in common that I did not, *they were all able to continuously focus upon what they wanted, not what they didn't want.*

The "your life is a garden" metaphor is one of my favorite ways to illustrate this point. If your life were a garden, you would want a garden with only pretty flowers in it, right? You wouldn't want a garden full of weeds, at least most people wouldn't. However, if there were weeds in this garden, how would you get them out? In this particular garden, the weeds are unpaid bills, debt, bad health, unhappy relationships, and anything else you don't want. The problem is that people try to pull them out by force. However, when you try to pull them out, they only become stronger. I recently heard someone say one of my favorite phrases, "Where your attention goes, your energy flows."

Your attention is the water—the garden is your life. You only want to water the flowers, which represent good health, a happy relationship, abundant finances, a fun career, and a nice home. You water the flowers by putting your attention upon the things that you desire. The only way to get rid of the weeds is by starving them out. You do this by simply not watering them with your attention. Very simple.

So, when you get home and open the mail to find bills and get really upset and frustrated, you have just watered the weeds. If you take a moment, sit down on the couch, relax, and visualize yourself on a tropical island taking a one-month vacation, completely carefree, you have just watered the flowers. If you go into the bathroom and find that your husband just left the toilet seat up again, and get upset because this happens all the time no matter what you say about it, you have just watered the weeds. If you visualize yourself with your partner, smiling and laughing, then you have just watered the flowers. If you feel helpless, at the whim of circumstances outside of your control and in a no-win situation, then you are continuously watering some deadly weeds. If you decide it's time to start focusing upon what you want in life and take charge of where your attention goes, then you are getting ready to create the ultimate flower garden of prosperity!

≋ 51 ≋

Visualization

V ISUALIZATION, IN AND of itself, can also be a standalone tool if you become good enough at it. The clearer the mental picture is in your mind, the more quickly you will manifest the visualized outcome. Your best results from visualization will come from small short time periods spent visualizing a scenario that symbolizes the successful completion of your manifestation. *In other words, if you wanted to manifest a new mate or life partner, you would spend a minute or two visualizing yourself with this other person. Ideally, the scenario would be representative of already having this happy successful relationship. If you visualize yourself just meeting this person, then you may only just meet them and never actually become intimate.* You may even only bump into them. However, if you visualize yourself happy and smiling together on a hike in the mountains, holding hands, you are virtually guaranteed of that outcome.

As you get better at visualizing, you will soon see how quickly and accurately your manifestation comes to fruition. I have never personally been that good at visualization, so I use pictures to help me. If there is something I really want to manifest and I need to get a visual image to help me speed up the process, I will search through magazines until I find the picture that most closely represents what I want. Then I put the picture on my manifestation board, which is just a cork bulletin board I have for the specific purpose of getting clear on what I want. I will spend a little time throughout the week meditating upon the picture until I manifest it in my life. I will also use the textures, smells, and sounds to assist in the visualization process. The more different sensations you can bring into your manifestation will also speed up the process as well.

≣ 52 ≣

Consistency Equals Results

WHEN IT COMES to allowing your manifestation to come to you, consistency will equal results. Abraham, from Abraham/Hicks Publications, calls it "The Art of Allowing," and this is really true because it *is* an art. You could also call it "The Art of Non-Resistance" with equal accuracy. You are really just mastering the ability of not resisting your own highest good. It is astonishing to realize how many ways you can and will resist your own best interests.

Anyone can experience being optimistic, believing in something or focusing on what they want for a minute or two. The challenge is in your ability to do this consistently throughout the day in your day-to-day life. If you decide you want to manifest a billionaire venture capitalist who wants to fund your new business idea, you would start with stating your intent. So you say with conviction and enthusiasm, "I want to meet a billionaire venture capitalist who wants to invest in my business idea." Next, you decide to visualize yourself shaking hands with this person and thanking them for their support in your business. At this point, you are well on your way to manifesting this outcome.

The real work may come later, after you've spent four or five days visualizing and still no manifestation. Typically, this stage of the process is where most people begin to sabotage their manifestation. Here are a few of the ways that you might sabotage yourself:

1) You begin to doubt whether or not you are really worthy of having something so great happen to you.

2) You begin to doubt that this process will work for you, you may wonder if it is unrealistic.

3) You suddenly change your mind or wonder if you should be doing something else instead.

4) You begin to worry that it will take too long and you lose your focus.

5) You suddenly fear that you are unprepared to receive this manifestation at all (this usually has to do with Number 1, worthiness. However, it can also have to do with feeling like you are physically unprepared, or do not have the skill set to meet the demands of this amazing manifestation.)

6) You make the mistake of listening to other people's ideas and limiting beliefs about your intended manifestation.

Ideally, if you have done the work at the beginning of this book, you will already have removed some of these potential obstacles and self-sabotaging mechanisms. But even if you find yourself grappling with these distractions, just remain consistent and stay detached from the outcome, while allowing your manifestation to show up in its own time and in its own way. If you do this, you *will* manifest your desired outcome. Remember, consistency equals results. Any time you allow yourself to think in limited or negative terms, you may slow down or halt your manifestation. Therefore, it is well worth the effort to become disciplined in your approach to manifestation. Doing so will reap amazing results!

Key Points

✓ You are deserving and worthy of having whatever you want. You do not need to justify or rationalize wanting whatever it is that you want. Try saying out loud to yourself, "I am deserving and worthy of the life of my dreams!" If it doesn't feel good to say this, that is a sure indicator that you still have some release work to do on your deserving and worthiness issues. Use the emotional release technique in this book to focus on releasing any feelings around this issue.

✓ You are not doing penance for any sort of karmic retribution from a past lifetime, or even this lifetime. Your point of power is in this moment, right here and now. From this moment, all the power of creation rests in the palm of your hand to create your reality exactly the way that you want it. You are free to create whatever you want! Say out loud to yourself: "I am now free to do whatever I want with my life!" It's true.

✓ Detach from seeing the outcome of your intended manifestation. Do this by staying focused upon what you want, not what you don't want. In any moment throughout the day, you can always stop and ask yourself "What am I focused upon in this moment?" This does not mean staying focused upon the outcome of your intended manifestation. Rather this means not allowing yourself to get drawn into negative circumstances while in the process of expecting and allowing your manifestation. For example, if you are in traffic and become irritated, don't allow it to bother you. Doing so will lower your vibrational rate of attraction and can even interfere with your intended manifestation, even though it may seem unrelated.

✓ If you are unclear about what you want to create in your life then a great starting point is by figuring out what you don't want. Make a list of all the things you don't want in your life. Then, figure out what the opposite of each one of those things looks like. Remember to go above and beyond—do not simply write down, "A relationship with no disagreements," or "All my bills paid." That won't cut it and will, in fact, get you focused again upon what you do not want. Instead, you would write, "A happy harmonious relationship" or "A new house and a vacation in Maui." This way you do not mistakenly end up focusing again upon what you do not want. Also, be specific about what you want. The more specific and detailed you are, the quicker your manifestation.

✓ Be consistent, create a routine every day where you spend some time focused upon what you want in your life. Start your day with meditation, then affirmation, then a one minute visualization focusing upon your desired manifestation. For example, my personal routine is twenty minutes meditation, followed by five minutes of affirmations, and ending with a 60-second visualization. Starting your day with meditation is the surest way to keep yourself centered, grounded, non-reactive, and will solidify your Reality Creation.

≋ 53 ≋

Taking Action

"**T**AKING ACTION" IS the third and final step in the Art of Manifestation. You may mistakenly believe that you do not need to take any action whatsoever to manifest something in your life. This belief stems from a misinterpretation about all the information circulating through the masses right now about manifestation. Two great movies have recently come out: *What the Bleep Do We Know!?* and *The Secret*. The greatest thing about these movies is that they help you to realize that anything is possible, that there is a way to effect change in your life and live your dreams. However, you may be under the mistaken impression that all you need to do is sit around all day, meditating and visualizing, and focusing upon things.

If, when your manifestation arrives, you do not take action, you will not achieve your desired outcome. You might be confusing the concept of manifestation with the concept of an Earth Master, or somebody who can literally create with a mere thought about something. You may have experimented around with small stuff like manifesting parking spots in the front of the grocery store. You may have even gotten pretty good at it, and always get your front spot by *visualizing* it or *feeling* it. You might be in the first stages of creating a faulty belief system, however, if you are thinking that all you needed to do is sit around and think about it. You see, you are and already have been taking the action of looking for parking spots every single day. Quite likely, if you are using the power of manifestation to create a parking space in front of a store, you are doing it on the way to wherever it is that you are going. You are literally in the process of taking action.

≡ 54 ≡

When The Lead Comes, Act On It

THE UNIVERSE WILL always deliver what you want. What you may not realize is that nothing can happen without your acting upon it. You *must* take action to gain the support of the Universe. The Universe will bring you what is referred to as the "lead." *The lead is the beginning of the opportunity that the Universe gives you so that your manifestation can come to fruition. When you put the intention to manifest out into the Universe, you have set the mechanics of manifestation into motion. As long as you do not cancel your order and put out a different signal, it will come to you. Then, how it comes to you is* not up to you.

The lead could be any of the following:

- ✦ An out of the blue idea to call someone.
- ✦ A sudden feeling to go to a certain event or place.

- A stranger bumping into you in line somewhere that strikes up a conversation with you.
- A phone call from someone with the opportunity you were looking for.
- An unexpected letter in the mail.
- A chance encounter on a plane flight.
- Anything at all, anywhere, at any time.

Pay attention, be ready, and when the moment comes, *act*!

≋ 55 ≋

The Universe Favors
a Body in Motion

A S CHANCE FAVORS the prepared mind, the Universe favors a body in motion. When you sit around waiting for something to happen, your energetic field begins to stagnate. When you get out into the world, you provide the Universe with multiple channels to deliver your manifestation to you and keep your energy flowing. The more you sit around wishing, hoping, and wanting something to happen, the more your opportunities will dry up. Now, not only has your energy stagnated and opportunities dried up, but on top of that you have probably cancelled out your manifestation with the energy of depression and yearning. Both of those emotions are devastating to your ability to purposefully create what you want.

Instead of sitting around intending to manifest something, state your intent to manifest what you want, then get on with your life. If you are attempting to manifest a new job, state your intent to manifest it then begin the process of looking for your job. If you are attempting to find your ideal partner for your dream relationship, state your intent to manifest them then begin your search. If you do not get out into the world, the Universe may not have the necessary channels to deliver to you what you want.

Another common fallacy is the idea that the Universe will just deliver large sums of money to you. It's true that if you believe it enough and are clear enough about it, you can manifest whatever you want. However, there is a deep driving desire within each and every one of us to contribute our unique talents and gifts to the world. *Your wealth and abundance will manifest at the intersection of your greatest joy and your unique contribution. When you are really excited about what you are doing, there will be a demand for what you have to offer.*

If you are just trying to manifest a large sum of money for the sake of having money, it's quite possible that you are doing this because you do not believe you have a unique contribution to offer the world. It's also possible that you have not found something to be passionate about. Now, there is nothing wrong with going for it if you want to try manifesting winning the lotto or manifesting a large check in the mail. However, you should only do this if you are really super-duper excited about it. If it doesn't get you all fired up, then it won't bring you abundance. *Whatever it is that gets you really excited and sounds like a lot of fun probably holds the key to your unlimited abundance!*

≋ 56 ≋

Avoid Unnecessary Action

O N THE OTHER hand, proper use of the process of manifestation will help you avoid unnecessary action and energy expenditure. You may be doing the exact opposite of the person who is sitting around meditating and visualizing all day. Instead, you may be running around in circles obsessing about achieving something. Regardless, this type of activity will have the same non-productive effect on your intended manifestation. Not only will you be canceling out your own good, you will also be energetically draining yourself. When you run around trying to achieve something, you are definitely not harnessing the unlimited power of manifestation. You are actually nullifying this power by taking too much action because at some level you believe it is up to you to get this thing done. In this case, you are trying to assume the job of the Universe itself.

I remember when I was at the point where I was re-establishing my personal training business in Los Angeles, California, after moving back from the Midwest. I needed to get things going, so I came up with the brilliant idea of signing up all the people in the surrounding office buildings next to the gym for two free personal training sessions. Much like a neurotic gerble running nonstop on a wheel, I ran around all day chasing people in the nearby office buildings, trying to get them to sign the form I'd created for free personal training sessions. It was hot outside; I was drained and had been kicked out of about half the offices I'd walked into. However, I felt for *sure* that this was a great idea and I would be booked solid, no problem! I remained optimistic about my idea and managed to get nearly 100 people signed up for two free sessions. *100 people!?* If you are personal trainer, you know that you only need 20 to 30 people to make incredible money. I just knew that I was on my way to the big time and already envisioned myself in a new twin turbo Porsche.

The first thing that happened was that most of the people I'd scheduled for free sessions were no-shows. One day I spent literally seven hours waiting around for people who didn't even bother to call and let me know they weren't going to make it. The second thing that happened was, of all the people who did show up for their free sessions, not one signed up for continued training. What I didn't realize was that I was promoting a free product, so instead of getting people really interested in personal training, I got all the people who liked getting things for free. My lesson was to value my time and energy by learning not to expend them uselessly!

I see many people in sales doing this, chasing down every single lead and coming home exhausted at the end of the day. After a few years, they are so energetically depleted of vital life force that they have developed chronic aches and pains and their body has begun to deteriorate. This is completely different from being on fire with your passion. I see Anthony Robbins or Oprah Winfrey as people who are on fire with their passion. They are both slam-packed to the hilt with their itineraries, but the passion for what they are doing infuses them with vital life energy. Also, the incredible income that results from combining their unique gift with their unique contribution sustains them and keeps them nourished. Anybody, including YOU, can do this. Period.

Trusting that you will receive the lead will help you to preserve your energy field and become more efficient. *After you've taken all the necessary steps, all you have to do is keep doing what you are doing and relax.* You may now release your manifestation to the Universe, knowing that it will come to you in its own time and in its own way. Your only assignment at this point is to be mindful that you do not cancel out your order by dwelling upon negative outcomes or doing anything else that lowers your vibrational energy field. If your life in this moment is depressing and you need to keep your mind off that feeling, do something fun that takes your mind off your present circumstance.

There are a many ways to do this. I, myself, like to read a good book; it's also something I was able to do when I was completely broke and out of work. I loved movies, but they cost money I didn't have. It gave me great pleasure to go into the bookstore and either buy a book that would last me for a few days, or simply read it in the bookstore without buying it. Obviously, I am completely against the idea of freeloading off bookstores and the diligent writers of the world who need us to pay for their books so they can make a living. Nowadays, I buy tons of books, but I am able to do so *because* I manifested more money into my life. Part of the process of manifesting funds in my life was to read books to keep my mind off my present circumstance. After I had money, I went back and paid for every single book I'd read that helped me stay detached from the bleak picture my life had been.

Key points
- ✓ At some point you will need to take action.
- ✓ If you do not know what you want to do with your life, sitting around thinking about it won't help. Instead, take some form of action. Get some exercise, look at job ads, go window shopping, anything that keeps you active. A certain amount of meditation and contemplation are good, but not all day.
- ✓ If everything is in place and you have taken the necessary steps, then relax. At this point you may need to take your mind off of your intended

manifestation and do something fun instead. Dwelling upon your present problem 24/7 will only keep you focused upon what you don't want. There is a difference between being motivated to change versus obsessing over something that you can do nothing about. Do not burn yourself out with unnecessary action or drive yourself crazy with ceaseless thought.

≋ 57 ≋

Creating The Ultimate
Life For Yourself

HOW DO YOU create the ultimate life for yourself? What do you like to do? What do you want to have? It can be an overwhelming question, but you are now ready to take a giant leap and go for it. I suggest you make a list of all of the things that get you really excited, all the way back to childhood. Next, cross reference this list with another list, a list of things you are really good at or that other people feel you are good at. This is different from Dad wanting you to become a family doctor or Mom always telling you that you look like Sean Connery. Instead, the list you want here is your own list of natural talents. So now you have two lists: one of things you love to do and another of the areas where you have natural talent. How do you combine them? There is always a way, you just have to be creative.

So many of the most successful people in the world today are successful as a result of knowing that they are able to create their own reality in their own way. It's okay—I now give you permission to create your own little world, too! Heck, make it huge if you want! Every single thing you see around you is the result of one person's idea. Every business, every film, every logo, beverage, food item, car, song... every table, every street name, is a result of one person's idea. Each one of these things comes from the mind of someone who broke free from the idea of limitation. All of these things together exist as a multitude of ideas from all the people of the world.

At this point, you've just got to get excited, because you are starting to realize that you really can create yourself anew at any moment. All you have to do is figure out what gets you really, really excited! Now, you're pumped because you have decided you are going to pursue something that's fun. Do you quit your job? Nope. You keep on taking action and allow the passion and enthusiasm of your new idea to begin to take seed. You start by figuring out exactly what it is that you want and state your desire to manifest it. Then you allow it to happen. Then, when the lead comes, if it's time to quit your job, you do so. However, the lead will tell you what to do and how to go about it. The Universe will provide for you the steps necessary to achieve your manifestation.

You can be, do, build, have, see, feel, or experience whatever you want, no questions asked. You have that power, it lies within you. If you do this work, you will learn how to unlock your ability to consciously create your reality. You are already a Master, you just haven't been aware of it. This is it, this is your life. Make it the best of the best, go for it and achieve your dreams. It's okay if the ride has been bumpy, you were just unaware of the fact that you can and have been paving your own road. Now that you're in control again, you can repave or even change the direction of the road. Pave a road that leads to your beautiful new house in the country! Pave a road that leads to the land of abundance and prosperity! Put some yellow bricks in it and head to the Emerald City if you like! This is your dream, your canvas, so paint your life the way you want it to look. Use all the colors you can think of to add richness and texture to the beautiful painting that is your life.

≋ 58 ≋

The Master Creator

WHEN YOU COMBINE and utilize all the tools of manifestation together, you can weave your life as if it were a beautiful tapestry. Each and every one of you has a unique contribution to make to the people of the world. There is nothing you cannot do if you are willing to take the time to learn how to utilize your latent ability of manifestation. When you meditate, affirm your manifestation, and visualize yourself living exactly the way you want to, it will happen just like that. As you do these things, your awareness will grow and you will strengthen your vibrational energetic field.

Eventually, you will get to the point where the first thing you do in the morning when you wake up is to meditate and visualize how you want your day to be. As you flow through your day effortlessly, noticing how everything that you mentally constructed in the morning has come to pass just as you intended it, you will be mindful of all the people interacting around you. Your awareness of their unconscious reactivity and limited thinking will not bring judgment; rather it will bring a new sense of respect for what you have achieved. You will remember that they are where you were only a short time ago and you will look upon them with kindness and compassion, knowing that one day they will become awakened to their own inner power as you have.

You will now sense that you have a tendency to naturally gravitate towards the people who sustain and nourish your newly-elevated energetic field, and they in turn will gravitate towards you, as well. You will have arrived at the point where even less action is required than before to create what you want. Now, your merest thought will send tremendous forces into action. You will have become so powerful that you need only have the briefest thought about a person and they will call you within moments. You will be extremely careful, because every single thing you visualize comes to pass with amazing accuracy. You will not be fearful of your thoughts, though, because you will have done sufficient clearing and meditation work to release your emotional wounds. Thus, you will now be able to create on command only that which you desire.

At some level of awareness in the back of your mind, you will sense a profound shift in the way you live your life. Simultaneously, you will realize that you have not had one negative thought in a long time. You have not had one negative thought in so long that you have surpassed the *Karmic Wheel* or the *Law of Action and Reaction.* As a result, your harnessing powers will be unsurpassed and you will realize the new abilities that mankind is just waking up to. You will have achieved ultimate power, as you literally have mind over matter.

*As a Master Creator, all of your heart's desires have been fulfilled and you have had the opportunity to experience every single thing you have ever wanted. The spontaneous realization occurs that it is time to for you to dedicate your mastery towards the betterment of the Earth. And, sure enough, you effortlessly manifest all of the people, places, and resources necessary to effect a higher level of change in the world than you ever dreamed possible. You are now a channel for higher energies and the realization sets in that the less you **think**, the more you **know**. You feel now as if all you have to do is simply exist and bask in the glory of a continuous streaming state of **Nowness**. You experience one moment of indescribable bliss after another. The idea of entertaining even one negative thought is so far removed from your Reality Creation that you have forgotten what it means to think in limited terms. For you, the illusion of limitation has fallen away so long ago that you barely even remember it.*

You spontaneously achieve total harmony in every area of your life, whether it be finance, relationship, career, mental clarity, or emotional freedom. Your life is your spiritual practice and you realize the age old adage that you are truly a spiritual being having a human experience. God has always been within you and is indeed you—and now you know this from the ultimate point of knowingness, that of the experiential. The answer has been with you all along.

≋ 59 ≋

Modern Day Reality Creationists

D URING THE CURRENT times of great stress and tension in the world, it is possible that you may find it becoming more difficult to positively affect your Reality Creation. It may seem to you, perhaps, that even trying to purposefully manifest and create something is becoming a bit of a task. Some amongst you have already mastered your ability to create on command and are unaffected by this tension and chaotic energy. However, for those people still learning to master their Reality Creation, it can be somewhat challenging to do so during this particular time period in history. And yet, there is no greater time than now to learn how to purposefully manipulate your own energy to create peace and prosperity for yourself and all those around you. Every time you master another lesson, all the people around you will also benefit from your efforts.

As you learn and master the lessons in this book, as well as anything else that elevates your conscious awareness, you will become a sea of calm in the midst of massive upheaval and turbulence. You will become the eye of the hurricane and more people will be drawn unto you. The rewards for completely mastering the energy that you are putting out into the world will manifest as your outer experience, and will reflect as all of your dreams coming to life in the physical. Events in the world at large will not affect you as you elevate your vibrational energetic field. When you get to a certain level, your energetic field will be so highly and positively charged that you can literally transmute other's people's negative unconscious energy by your mere presence. This is why now is the time to do the work and become self aware, because you are needed to help us enter a new world of magic and creativity.

God bless and enjoy creating the life of your dreams!

≡ Q & A with the author ≡

What's different about Reality Creation 101?!

What's different about Reality Creation 101 is that it is written by someone who went through all of the painful lessons on how not to create the life of your dreams. Reading this book can and will help you prevent all of the pitfalls inherent in learning how to manifest and purposefully direct your thoughts. You will learn about your unconscious and how you may be continuously sabotaging your own best efforts at change. You will learn how to heal your unconscious limiting beliefs and emotional wounds.

Who the heck are you? What makes you such an expert on manifestation?

I am the walking manifestation of the path of empowerment. I arrived at this destination by way of learning everything that I am not. I am an expert at manifestation because I started from a place of not being able to purposefully manifest anything. I am every man, woman, and child that ever dreamed of living the life of their dreams. I am every soul that wanted to experience a life with no limits. Through ultimate disempowerment I have learned ultimate empowerment.

Yes yes yes, but I've heard it all before!

Yes, but you've never been given all of the tools before. This is not a think positive and become rich book. This is a book on mastery, helping you to master your own inner domain in order to create whatever you want.

But wait, aren't I creating my reality right now???

Indeed, you are. In fact, you are never not creating your reality. It is simply the difference between conscious reality creation and unconscious reality creation, or purposefully creating what you want vs. creating a default reality based upon your repressed emotional energy.

What about relationships? What about love?

It's all in there. As you work towards healing your unconscious you will become more magnetic to the things that you truly want in life. Instead of trying to fight your way out of the vicious cycles that you find yourself trapped in, you can allow yourself to be gently elevated above them. The more you do this work on yourself, the higher the version of yourself that you will attract to yourself.

Are you talking about mirroring?

Absolutely. Everything and everyone in your reality is only part of you that you are mirroring out to them.

Your mate or life partner is the most extreme and accurate version of this. When you elevate yourself and do the work in *Reality Creation 101*, you will become a higher version of yourself. As you become a higher version of yourself you will be magnetic to a partner that mirrors a higher version of yourself. This is good.

Will this book make me rich?

Is that what you want? Everyone says they want to be rich. But, more likely than not you just want to be happy and have abundance. Probably an even better word is fulfillment. You want to be fulfilled and have abundance in every area of your life.

But what if I really, really want to be rich?

Then the tools in this book can be used to create that as well. If you master the tools in this book then there is nothing that you cannot do.

Do manifestation techniques differ for material and spiritual needs?

A clever question. Indeed, the techniques are one and the same for both material and spiritual needs. In fact, utilizing these techniques will alter and even augment your perception of reality. This, in turn, will lead to greater self awareness which will lead to integrating the fragmented aspects of your psyche. And, in turn, as you integrate the fragmented aspects of your psyche you move closer to Oneness. This is the ultimate goal of every Soul, whether they are conscious of it or not.

What happens to the manifestation process in the year 2012?

The year 2012 is purported to be the year of critical mass, or the year in which we reach the total acceleration of consciousness. In theory, as we approach this time period, we will see a speeding up of the "thought, word, deed" process. Another way to look at this is that your thoughts will become things more quickly. 2012 is theoretically the year at which we reach instantaneous manifestation, or in which we become one with our thoughts.

How does one naturally distinguish between mood making and positive thinking?

"Mood making" implys that we are in conscious control of our mood, which is not the case. In general, if you are feeling moody then you are not conscious of your thoughts. However, it should also be noted, that emotionality is a natural occurrence of the human being and should be allowed to be expressed. One might even say that an actual *mood* only occurs when we resist our emotions. In other words, what you resist will persist.

Positive thinking is the purposeful focusing of ones thoughts on things that make them feel good. This is all well and good as long as it does not put you in a state of resistance to your natural need to express your emotions. If you are feeling sad about something, then perhaps you need to feel sad. If you need to express this emotion of sadness and instead decide to focus upon a positive thought, you may end up repressing the sadness which will only create greater sadness for you in the future. Conversely, if you are perpetually sad, then it may be time to attempt to redirect your thoughts into a positive, higher vibrational state of mind.

If the law of attraction is vibrational, and we are in a bad mood, we are attracting negative vibrations...how does one break it without faking it? Actually shift ones thinking and vibrational frequency?

This is the crux of this book, to shift yourself vibrationally speaking, into a higher state. If a person is in what we term a "negative emotion", or is simply not feeling very good, then in order to elevate their vibrational state of being they will need to do one of two things. They will need to either release and allow their negative emotions or begin to focus upon positive thoughts. I recommend doing both. If you release and allow your emotions to *be* then you are naturally in a state of non-resistance. This is superior to repressing your negative emotions and trying to focus upon a positive thought. This will create resistance in the process and will energetically drain you. It can be done this way, but now you will be in a perpetual battle to keep yourself elevated because you are still holding onto lower vibrational emotions within your bio-energetic sphere. In this case you have become like a ship that raises it's sails and lowers it's anchor at the same time. Releasing the negative emotions first will allow you to pull up the anchor, then focusing upon the positive thoughts will raise the sails.

⇛ A note from the author ⇚

I T HAS BEEN reminded to me many times, that life is not a destination-it is a journey. And, within this journey I continue to evolve and grow. I do not strive to be perfect, but I do strive to be excellent. I, like everyone else, have my moments(and sometimes days) of unconscious reactivity. I suffer physical and emotional pain just like the next person. However, the more I do the work, the more I do these exercises, truly the less I suffer. And, the more powerful I become. I'm very excited to share with you what has worked for me.

≋ Bio ≋

CHRISTOPHER A. PINCKLEY was born in Shawnee Mission, KS on May 5th 1971. His parents were very migratory and so he lived in many areas throughout the United States while growing up. Much of his family remained in Lincoln, NE and so this ended up becoming his home town.

As a personal trainer and rehabilitation specialist, Christopher became interested in alternative healing modalities. His primary impetus was healing his own chronic knee pain and his torn shoulder. Later, he developed chronic fatigue syndrome and some metabolic problems as well. This propelled him forward to continue studying Eastern Medicine as well as alternative mind/body therapies.

Christopher now resides in the East Bay of San Francisco where he does spiritual consulting for clients as well as working on his book series.

Made in the USA
Lexington, KY
06 March 2012